HAL LEONARD
BASS METHOD

JAZZ BASS
BY MATTHEW RYBICKI

PHOTOS BY MEG RYBICKI PHOTOGRAPHY

Speed • Pitch • Balance • Loop

To access audio visit:
www.halleonard.com/mylibrary

Enter Code
8861-3201-4323-1384

ISBN 978-1-4950-4456-4

Visit Hal Leonard Online at
www.halleonard.com

Contact Us:
Hal Leonard
7777 West Bluemound Road
Milwaukee, WI 53213
Email: info@halleonard.com

In Europe contact:
Hal Leonard Europe Limited
42 Wigmore Street
Marylebone, London, W1U 2RN
Email: info@halleonardeurope.com

In Australia contact:
Hal Leonard Australia Pty. Ltd.
4 Lentara Court
Cheltenham, Victoria, 3192 Australia
Email: info@halleonard.com.au

INTRODUCTION

...ny hope that this book will be a compelling guide for your progress along the path of musical expression with ...strument in the world: the drums.

...g, of course. Who would want to play the drums when the bass exists?!

...we're often the underdogs in an ensemble, we all know the power and responsibility that the bass holds. And in this ...zing art form called "jazz," that power and responsibility is profound.

...While there are many, many branches of this tree to examine, in this book, I want to primarily focus on the practical role of the instrument in traditional, or "straight-ahead," jazz. And, as an example of the problem with simple labels, even these parameters can't summarize the variety of music that encompasses what's contained within straight-ahead itself.

Nonetheless, we have to start somewhere, and it's my belief that mastering the fundamentals is critical to successfully achieving our ultimate goal: an expression of our experience of the human condition in musical terms. Simply put, we want to communicate with one another.

My goal is to provide you with information that should help you to develop the tools to share your expression. The function of these lessons is to focus your innate musicality into tangible exercises that will allow you to experience measurable progress, and apply that progress in real ways as soon as you are able. I have tried to emphasize some concepts that aren't often discussed in method books in the hopes of providing you with a unique perspective that you may not typically encounter.

Each chapter is divided into six parts that alternate between concepts and performance:

1. **Living in Harmony:** Learn how to construct chords of all kinds.
2. **Technique Tune-Up:** Review or discover techniques specifically important to jazz.
3. **Changes Are Inevitable:** Explore common chord progressions and learn about chord functions.
4. **Bass Accompaniment:** Investigate a variety of ways that the bass acts as an accompaniment instrument.
5. **Preparing to Solo:** Practice scales that fit with the chapter's specific harmonic examples.
6. **All Ears on You:** Consider a variety of concepts and techniques related to soloing.

There is literally a lifetime of learning in this music, and no single book can encapsulate all that we need to learn. I do hope, however, that this book can be a useful aid in your journey.

To that end, I've found it helpful to separate musical challenges into two discrete categories: 1) technique and 2) content. Another way to think about this is: "*How* to play" and "*What* to play."

We'll explore these in the following chapters, but keep this general idea in mind: If you encounter a problem, ask yourself if this is an issue of technique or content. *Technique* encompasses everything from how to hold the bass to executing a complex solo at a high velocity. *Content* has to do with what note choices you decide to make in the moment, what musical vocabulary informs your melodic ideas, or what emotion you might be trying to represent. To put it more simply, knowing how to produce an accurate F note, in tune and in time, is a different skill than knowing when or where to play that note.

Because music isn't linear, however, we have the great fortune of being able to practice more than one thing at a time. So, please know that every sincere effort that you make to improve your musical ability informs everything about your musicianship. The work itself, whether you "succeed" at a lesson or not, will pay dividends in all of your musical efforts from that point on. Patient and diligent study will pay off, many times in ways that you never expected!

Along those lines, I must also mention that a lifetime of *listening* is absolutely crucial with respect to speaking the language of jazz. This can't be overstated. Truly, let your ears be your best and most important instructor. Listening to the masters of this music, from any era, and as much as possible, is supremely important. As I'm writing this, we lost one of the true legends and masters of the trumpet, Clark Terry. His life of creativity, passion, education, and swing made a lasting impact on countless musicians. And, as he famously said, learning to improvise is about *imitation*, *assimilation*, and *innovation*. To imitate masters of this music, we have to study those masters directly. So, again, listen to as much music as you possibly can. Let this be your primary goal.

It is my wish that your musical journey will be as rewarding as mine has been. Good luck, and have fun!

—Matthew Rybicki

WHAT IS THIS THING CALLED "JAZZ"?

Jazz is all around us. It has become part of the cultural DNA of the United States and has been exported to all areas of the globe. It's a living, breathing entity and the very nature of its creation ensures that it will never be the same twice. It is a rare gem in the world of musical expression—a way of playing that satisfies the head, the heart, and the feet. It's meant to be both visceral and sacred and, at its best, it succeeds brilliantly at both.

There are many ways in which these elements are brought out in the music, but let's take one common example: a quartet performance at a dimly-lit jazz club in the heart of Manhattan, at the height of a brisk and golden-leaved autumn. There is a tenor saxophone player, a pianist, a bassist, and a drummer. And they are *cookin'*!

They begin a song that you recognize. While the saxophone player states the familiar melody, the pianist plays carefully chosen notes that support the main theme. The bassist, standing between the pianist and drummer, plays a continuous series of notes that reinforce the composition. And the drummer helps to spur them all in waves of intensity.

As the saxophone player begins to solo, the melody suddenly becomes less recognizable. You may hear snippets of phrases that remind you of the tune, but now the solo veers this way and that, connecting one new idea to another. The pianist continues to carefully choose her notes, interjecting surprising rhythms that complement the saxophone player's melodies and further his ideas. And the bass player, with relentless stamina, creates phrase after phrase of uninterrupted notes that provide a foundation that's both solid and smooth.

Once the tenor finishes his improvised solo, the pianist takes her turn and executes exciting new melodies of her own that somehow remain tied to the original theme of the song…and on it goes.

What exactly is happening here? How are these musicians sounding so in sync with each other but seemingly "making it up as they go along"? In short, each musician has taken the years of individual practice, ensemble playing, careful study, and dedicated listening to master the ability to play their instrument at the highest level while crafting spontaneous compositions full of the language of the music.

Typically, there is an agreed upon form of a tune, which is a set number of measures with specific harmony and a specific melody—the basic song structure. Like the many floors of a skyscraper, the structural blueprint of the song remains constant and is repeated over and over, with new musical events happening in each moment. It's the song itself that keeps them all together, but they allow for the rooms on each floor of that blueprint to be filled with different things, which are created in the moment, while following the layout of the room.

From there, the musicians take turns being supported or being supportive. When one has their chance to be highlighted, each of the others works to help them express themselves.

Your role as the bassist is to provide a solid foundation of rhythm and harmony that plays a key role in keeping the band cohesive. You'll be relied upon for clear definition of time and harmonic movement, all the while interacting in a musical way with your bandmates. You'll have opportunities to solo, where you can express your interpretation of the song with clever melodies, and the others will support you in that moment. Most importantly, however, you must always be listening because jazz is ultimately a dialogue in which your respectful participation is necessary to move the "conversation" forward.

All of this is well within your reach as a musician. It's simply a matter of assembling many small ideas together into ever-increasing layers of complexity.

So, let's take individual steps along this path together. We'll explore four basic concepts—technique, harmony and theory, bass accompaniment, and soloing—in each of the upcoming chapters. Each chapter will build upon the last, with each having a unique, unifying song or idea as a vehicle to explore new concepts. Before you know it, you'll be swingin' with the best of them, and I hope that you will enjoy the journey getting there!

CHAPTER 1

LIVING IN HARMONY: INTERVALS & CHORDS

In a musical context, an **interval** refers to the distance between two pitches. Each interval has a specific name, and these names ultimately help to give identification to sound.

Intervals can be **melodic**—meaning the notes occur one after another—or **harmonic**, whereby the two pitches occur simultaneously.

For example, the distance between the notes F and C is a perfect 5th. Whether they are played together or not, the interval is still a perfect 5th.

The names for the intervals are derived from two things: the quality of the interval (major, minor, perfect, augmented, or diminished) and the number (2nd, 4th, 7th, etc.), or quantity, which is taken from numbers assigned to a scale.

The first note, or root, of the scale is 1. The second note in the scale is 2, and so on.

We attribute qualities like "major," "diminished," or "minor" to the specific relationship between the first and second note.

Individual Intervals in the F Major Scale

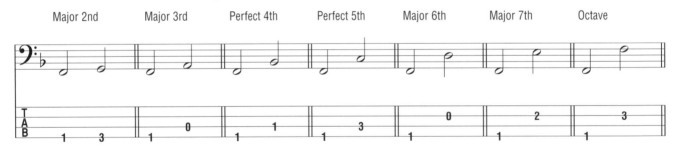

However, intervals refer to the relationship between any two pitches, not just from F, for example. Each pitch within the F major scale has a relationship (and interval name), just as any other two notes can be described with an interval.

In the example below, every interval is listed, starting from the note A.

For future reference, a major 2nd is often called a **whole tone** or **whole step**, and a minor 2nd is often called a **half tone** or a **half step**.

Let's play the melody to the popular hymn "Amazing Grace" and look at various ways to label different intervals. On the recording, I've taken some liberties with the rhythm, but the intervals remain the same. Notice that an interval exists between any two notes—they don't have to be side by side.

TRACK 1

AMAZING GRACE

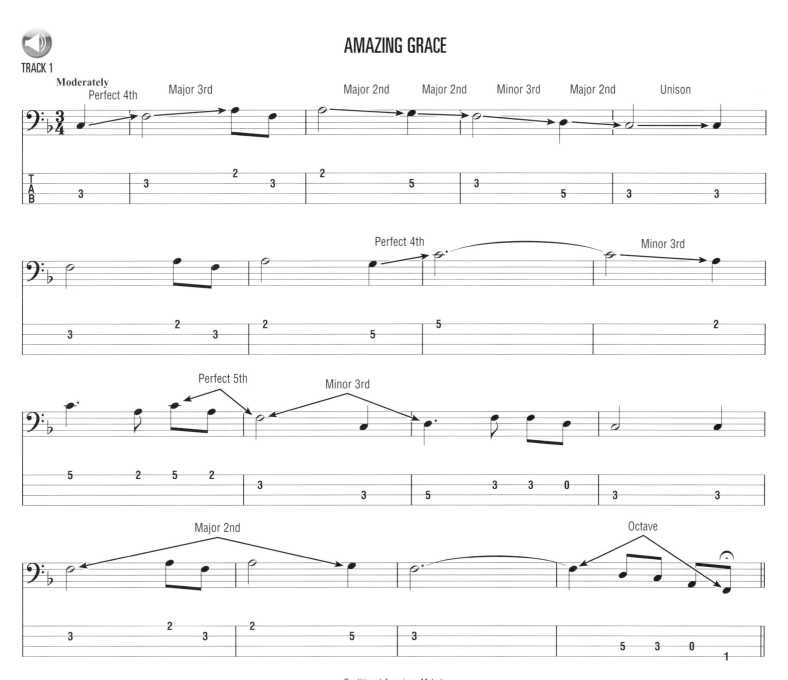

Chords are created when more than two notes are played at the same time. Like intervals, chords are also given qualities that indicate information about their sound. Triads are chords with three specific notes—a root, 3rd, and 5th—and there are four qualities that we use to name them: major, minor, augmented, and diminished.

Major triads have intervals that are the distance of a major 3rd and a perfect 5th away from the root of the chord. Their chord symbols are written with a single letter, which represents the root of the chord. Here are a few examples of major triads:

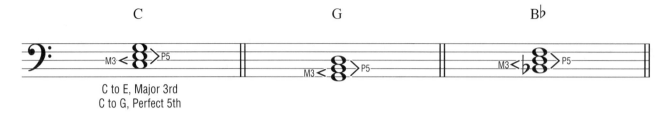

C to E, Major 3rd
C to G, Perfect 5th

Minor triads are comprised of minor 3rd (sometimes called a "flat 3rd") and perfect 5th intervals. Their chord symbols are normally written with the root letter of the chord and the suffix "m," but you may sometimes see them written with "min," "mi," or what looks like a minus sign: Gmin, Gmi, or G-.

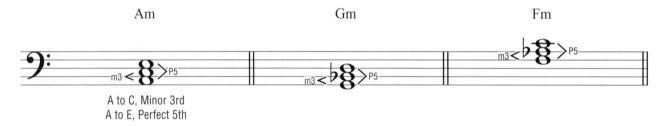

A to C, Minor 3rd
A to E, Perfect 5th

Augmented triads contain a major 3rd and an augmented 5th (sometimes called a "sharp 5") in relation to the root of the chord. Augmented triads are most often written with a combination of the root letter and a plus sign (+), but you may sometimes see the suffix "aug."

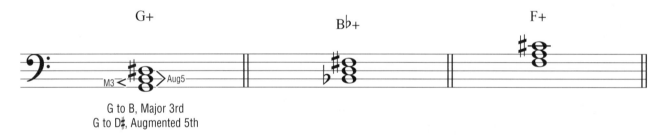

G to B, Major 3rd
G to D♯, Augmented 5th

Diminished triads are constructed with a minor 3rd and diminished 5th (sometimes called a "flat 5"). Their chord symbols contain the root letter and a small circle (°), but sometimes the symbol is replaced with the suffix "dim."

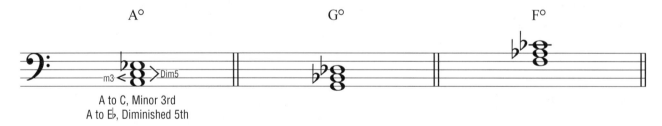

A to C, Minor 3rd
A to E♭, Diminished 5th

An **arpeggio** is the term used for playing the notes of a chord in succession. Rather than playing the notes simultaneously, the chord is "spelled out" one note at a time. Arpeggios directly outline the harmonies and are the springboard to creating solid, functional bass lines.

Below are the **diatonic triads** in the key of F major, arpeggiated in 3/4 time. Diatonic means all the notes belong to the same scale, or key.

Arpeggiated triads don't need to be played in a specific order, like root–3rd–5th; they can also be played as inversions, beginning with a chord tone other than the root. An arpeggio played up from the 3rd of the chord is called **first inversion**, while up from the 5th is called **second inversion**. Here are some examples with the starting note repeated at the top of the arpeggio:

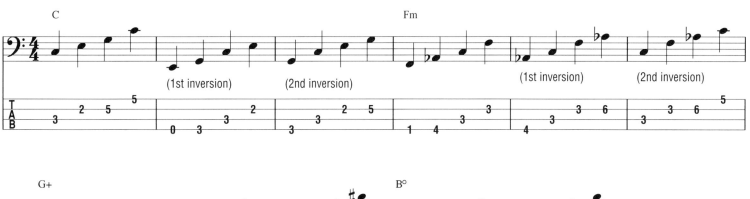

Let's return to "Amazing Grace." In the following exercise, you'll find the chord symbols written above the melody, which is on the top line. A bass line comprised entirely of arpeggiated triads that follow the chord changes is written on the staff below.

TRACK 2

Before moving on, take some time to identify the inversions used in the bass line above, and then get ready to explore our first section on technique.

TECHNIQUE TUNE-UP: GETTING A SOUND

The first thing that a listener hears when we are performing is our sound. No matter how musically experienced they are, any listener can process the quality of the sound that we project from the instrument.

Both upright and electric bassists have the option of a wide variety of electronic gear to enhance, manipulate, and boost their sound. Ideally, this gear should be used to support the natural tone, volume, and projection that we work to get from our instruments, so learning to produce our best unamplified sound first is key.

Some words that might describe a traditionally high-quality bass sound are "big," "warm," or "fat." To achieve these characteristics, both the plucking hand and the fretting hand come into play.

The fret-hand fingers should be curved so the strings can be pressed with the fingertips. On the double bass, use the weight of your arm (along with gravity) to help press the strings down onto the fingerboard, rather than gripping the neck with your hand muscles only.

You have more timbral options with your plucking hand. The broad idea is that no matter the plucking-hand shape or position, you should strive to keep as much "meat" of your finger(s) on the string. With more surface area on the string, you'll produce a louder and bigger sound. On the upright, practice playing with your index finger parallel to the string, drawing the string towards you as if you were drawing back an arrow in a bow.

One finger plucking

Two fingers together

Using two fingers simultaneously is more common with the upright than the electric bass. However, when you alternate two fingers on either instrument, work to keep as much of your finger on the string as is possible while still being able to maneuver through a musical phrase.

Conventional electric bass technique

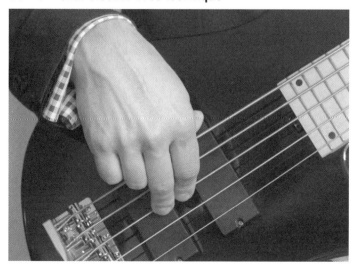

For electric, your index finger will be almost perpendicular to the string, using a slight angle to accommodate the disparate lengths of your index and middle fingers. This is most effective when your other fingers are closed into your palm. To achieve this, place a small object in your remaining three fingers to keep your technique disciplined.

Effective projection of our sound is crucial to being heard. Projecting our sound involves not only basic volume but also:

- A clear idea of the sound we want to express

- The technical aspects of creating that sound on the instrument

- Depth and "fullness" of the notes we are creating

- Accuracy of intonation

- Command of rhythm

- Facility on the instrument to execute a given statement

- Confidence in our musical intention

An unconventional approach to refining projection is to imagine, while you are practicing, that the sounds coming from your instrument are not only filling the room that you are in, but that you are "sending" those sounds through the walls, ceilings, and floors. While this idea generally applies to the double bass, you can apply the same concept to the electric. Even though the sound of the electric relies heavily on the pickups and amplifier, we still need to consider how we are getting the sound out of the instrument itself.

And because of the pickups, effects, and amplifier, there are even more subtleties that can be brought out in the sound of the bass. For example, one thing that we must learn to negotiate is the length of our notes.

Check out the graphic below, where we can take a closer look at the "envelope" of a note:

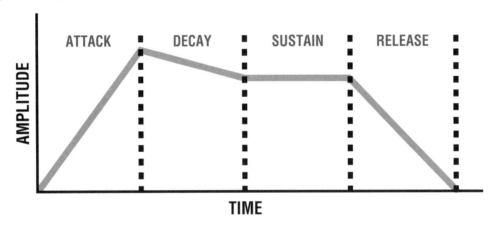

For our purposes, let's reduce the graphic above to simply **attack** and **decay** over the length of the note. In other words, how quickly the note sounds when you strike it (attack), and how quickly it fades afterward (decay).

This is important in jazz bass, especially on the electric bass, as the length of the notes *affects the perception of rhythm*. In a standard walking bass line, which is played with continuous quarter notes, there needs to be some separation between each note in order to maintain a defined pulse. If all of our quarter notes have a long decay, for instance, it becomes difficult for the listener to hear the rhythmic crispness necessary to maintain a good swing feel. Notes on a highly-amplified upright, or on an electric bass in general, tend to run together. This gives the quarter-note feel a "mushy" sound.

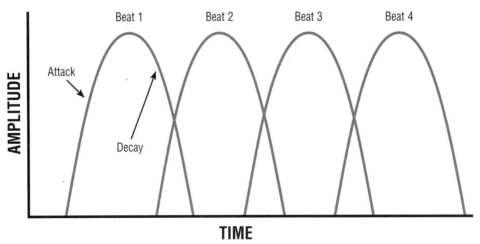

Can you see how the decay of one note runs into the attack of the next note? This makes distinguishing between the two notes more difficult, rhythmically. Below, you can see how shortening the length of the notes gives us more separation, helping to define the pulse.

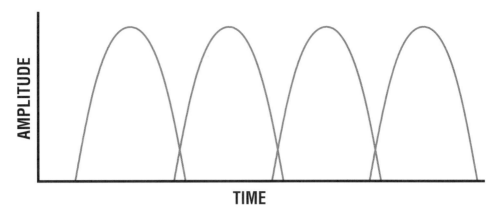

To manipulate the note length, first look at the string height, or action, of your bass. In general, higher action will provide a faster decay. Also important is the articulation of notes with your fretting hand; you should strive to control the duration and pressure with which you hold a given note. These tips apply to both electric and upright.

One specific tip to help you imitate an upright sound on electric is to dampen all strings with the side of your plucking hand while striking the strings with your thumb. This technique is called palm muting, and you can experiment with your palm at various distances from the bridge to control the length of the decay.

Apply these ideas and techniques to the previous playing examples in this chapter. When you are playing through the intervals and triads, keep your sound in mind. By making your sound a consistent priority throughout your practicing, you will quickly find the means to best express yourself.

CHANGES ARE INEVITABLE: INTRODUCTION TO CHORD PROGRESSIONS

A **chord progression** is a series of chords that move from one to another in time. Also called a "harmonic progression" or "chord changes," a chord progression can be as small as two chords taken out of context for study, or a complete sequence of chords that make up a composition. There is extraordinary value in grasping how the chords move and influence each other.

When we take a macro view of the chord progression within a piece of music, we're given the harmonic "blueprints" of the song. This allows us to maintain the structure of the composition itself as we create new melodies with our improvisation, and provides us with the symbols to analyze the relationships between the chords.

When analyzing, Roman numerals are used to indicate the function of a chord. The Roman numerals are sometimes followed by a suffix that tells us the chord quality, though this isn't always necessary. A conventional way to indicate major or minor without writing out the quality is to distinguish between uppercase and lowercase Roman numerals. Uppercase means major, and lowercase means minor.

Look at this analysis of chords diatonic to the key of F major:

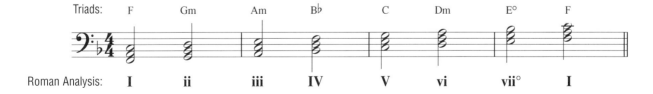

Now let's use Roman numerals to analyze the harmony of "Amazing Grace":

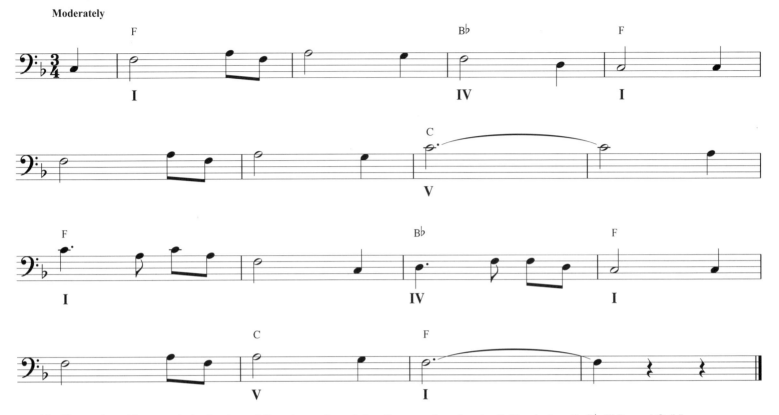

You'll see that this song is in the key of F major and contains three major chords: F (the I chord), B♭ (IV), and C (V).

There are several common chord progressions that reappear again and again in jazz, and so it's very helpful to become familiar with them. We'll cover new progressions in each upcoming chapter.

The first to consider are the chord-progression fragments that often occur in jazz compositions. The most ubiquitous fragment is V–I. We will explain in more detail in the next chapter why this is so, but for now, understand that it is a cadence; that is, a chord progression that creates a sense of resolution. Because of this, we say the V "resolves" to the I. Here are several examples of the V–I cadence:

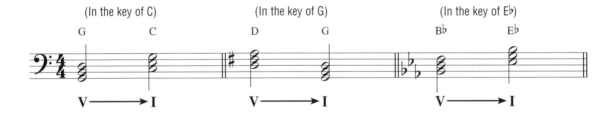

Another important, but less widely used, cadence in jazz is IV–I. This is the familiar "Amen" cadence in Western classical music. Although it's not used in jazz harmony as often as V–I, the underlying concept is very important to know.

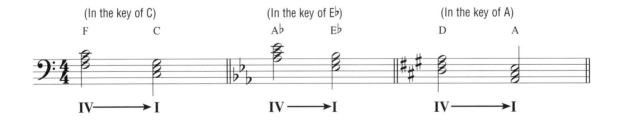

Now let's move on to this chapter's examination of the role of bass accompaniment in jazz.

BASS ACCOMPANIMENT: ROLE CALL

Over the years, the role of the bass in ensembles expanded in options, from pure accompaniment to "co-improviser" to lead melody. Today, we are expected to master the instrument in all of these ways and more. While it can be a challenge, I find it satisfying to have so many different ways to play.

However, the primary function of the bass in a standard jazz group remains the same: accompanying others. Yes, bass solos have become a standard part of group performances, but the vast majority of the time spent playing is still "comping." And doing this well is a talent that takes just as much effort, diligence, and dedication as learning how to improvise freely over an arrangement of a Wayne Shorter composition in 15/8 time.

These are distinct skills unique to the accompanist, and some are very specific to the bass itself. Precisely because bassists often are not highlighted, the skills most necessary to function well in an ensemble are overlooked. For example, it's human nature to want to "get to the good stuff," like playing a blistering solo of your very own, and disregard walking bass, but I encourage you to think differently.

No matter the situation, we want to have good intonation, good time, and substantial musical statements. We should strive for effortless control of our instruments, supple movements of melodies, and clever editing of our improvised ideas.

These are concepts that take serious dedication to master. Let's begin by reviewing the fundamentals of bass accompaniment.

Take a look at this bass line to an excerpt of "Amazing Grace":

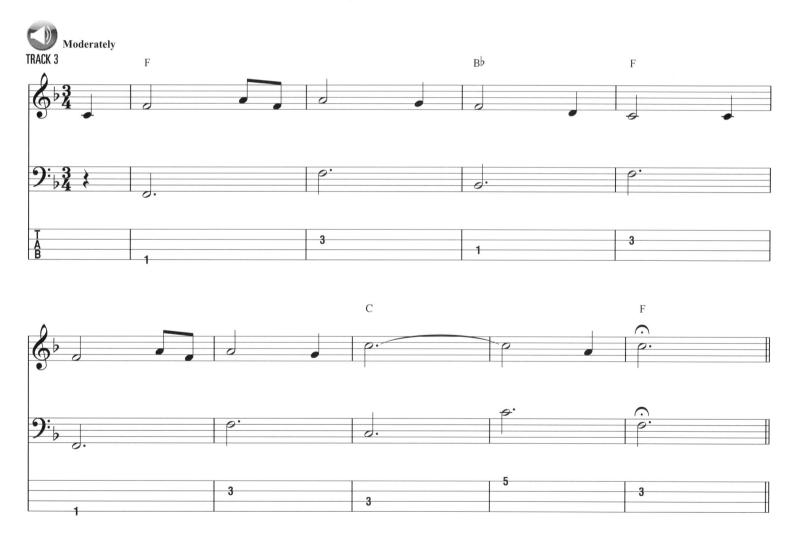

What do you notice?

If you observed that the bass part matched up with the roots of each chord on the downbeat of each chord change, you've got it. Despite the changing rhythm of the bass line, the first note of each bar is the root of the chord in that measure.

This basic idea is the keystone to building bass lines. When accompanying, part of our job as bassists is to "outline" the chord changes. This means that we are constantly reinforcing the harmony and harmonic progression by sticking close to the basic structure of each chord in our line.

Listeners and other ensemble members rely on the bass to help ground and identify the harmony.

Let's add more chords to the "Amazing Grace" progression and see how they affect the bass line.

TRACK 4

Moderately

Notice that the bass notes change with the new chords, while the rhythm of the line is exactly like the previous version. But even when the bass line is very active, we need to maintain a sense of rhythmic and harmonic support. In that regard, on the following page is "Amazing Grace" with a more active bass line that has roots on the downbeats of the chord changes, as well as other notes from each chord's triad.

We will explore these ideas and much more in greater depth in the chapters to come, but now it's time to look at our first section on gathering information in preparation for creating your own solo.

PREPARING TO SOLO: MAJOR AND PENTATONIC SCALES

Scales are created from a succession of intervals between a given note and its octave. One way to look at a major scale, for example, is to see it as a series of whole steps and half steps. A minor scale would have a different series of these intervals, in a different order. A diminished scale would have yet another combination, and so on.

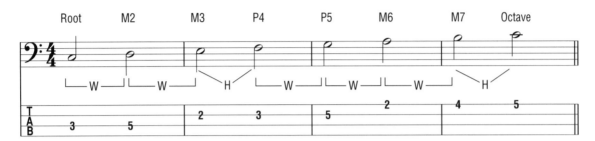

Personally, I find it easier to think of the list of intervals as they exist in relation to the root of the scale. From this perspective, a major scale has a major 2nd, major 3rd, perfect 4th, perfect 5th, major 6th, major 7th, and an octave.

As you probably already know, the sound and pattern of a scale can be applied to any of the 12 notes that we use in Western music. Here's the pattern applied to F:

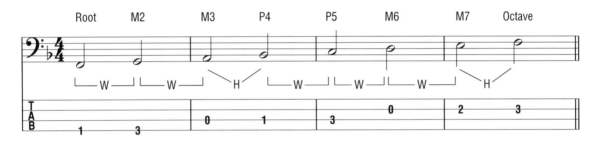

However you choose to view the pattern of notes in a scale, the important thing is to assimilate the sound and underlying pattern of the scale. That way, you can apply your knowledge to any note of a given chord. You will be expected to know all scales intimately, so be sure to internalize them in any and every way that you can.

Pentatonic scales are comprised of five notes instead of the typical seven or eight. Because there are fewer notes, they can be easily applied to a variety of situations. We will explore some of these later. But for now, let's look at their construction.

The scale numbers 1, 2, 3, 5, and 6 comprise the major pentatonic scale. This is essentially a smaller grouping of the full major scale, as reflected by these scale numbers. Here is the F major pentatonic scale:

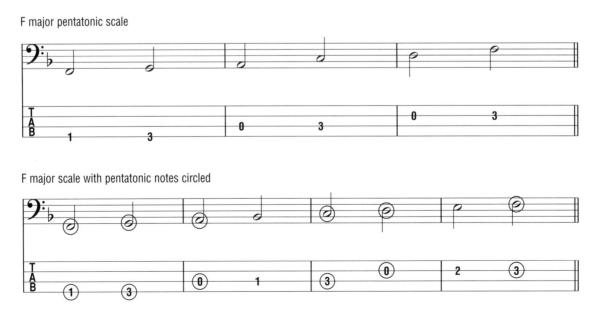

F major pentatonic scale

F major scale with pentatonic notes circled

And here are a few examples of the major pentatonic scale with other roots (but learn all 12!):

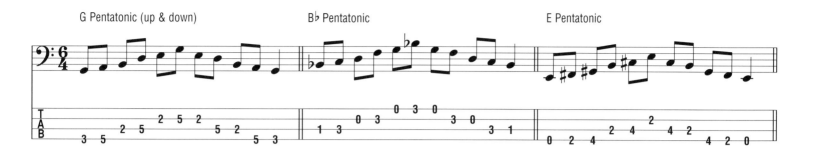

Play the melody to "Amazing Grace" again, but this time notice that one of the world's most famous melodies is based entirely on the F major pentatonic scale.

Now let's find out how we might use these scales in improvisation…

ALL EARS ON YOU: INTRODUCTION TO SOLOING

While the bass wasn't considered a solo instrument in jazz until around the 1940s, bassists have truly brought the instrument into a new space over time. Changes in technique, instrument setup, and even string and pickup technology have opened up sonic possibilities for the bass that weren't even previously imagined.

A key difference is that the instrument has been "released" from its functional role and allowed to freely explore melodies and rhythms, with the other band members contributing as accompanists and musical foils.

This freedom can seem daunting for us bass players who spend so much time and effort learning how to execute accompaniment for others in the best way possible. When our time comes to be free, we may feel intimidated (I certainly did, and sometimes still do!). But, the principles we've already been studying still apply. Harmonic and rhythmic fundamentals don't change just because we're now soloing; we are still striving to make cogent and meaningful musical statements. Our time feel, instrument's sound, and engagement with others on the bandstand are still critically important.

You should feel encouraged that you most likely already have all the necessary ingredients to express yourself in a conventional jazz solo! You just need to continue to get deeper into and expand your own knowledge, sound, and unique musical vision. But if you're brand new to improvisation, it's best to first set expectations, and then give yourself reasonable parameters in which to work.

One simple way to approach conventional soloing is by building variations on the melody of the song.

For example, here is "Amazing Grace" again, but this time we've expanded on the main melody. This could definitely be considered a solo chorus (a chorus is one time through the song form).

TRACK 6
Moderately

Where are these extra notes coming from? Well, I'm choosing the vast majority from the F major scale (the scale we just learned), as it generally fits all of the chords.

So, our parameters in the example above were to use the song "Amazing Grace" and play with and expand on the melody. Now let's create a new solo chorus over these chords, but this time our "rules" will be to only choose notes from the triads that comprise each chord, keeping the rhythms from the previous example basically the same.

TRACK 7

While this may not be the level of melodic sophistication that you're aiming for, keep in mind that setting up expectations and guidelines for yourself will allow you to focus on making progress amidst a vast ocean of options and information.

CHAPTER 2

LIVING IN HARMONY: MAJOR, MINOR, AND DOMINANT SEVENTH CHORDS

In jazz, we tend to use chords with more "ingredients" than triads. Seventh chords add one note that is an interval of a 7th above the root of a triad to form a four-note chord, and their sound is characteristic to the jazz style.

Major seventh chords are created with the root, 3rd, 5th, and 7th (1–3–5–7) of the major scale. You will see various suffixes used for their chord symbols, some of which are listed below.

	1	2	3	4	5	6	7	8
Cmaj7, CM7, C△7	C	D	E	F	G	A	B	C

Here are the notes of a C major seventh chord, arpeggiated and spanning two octaves:

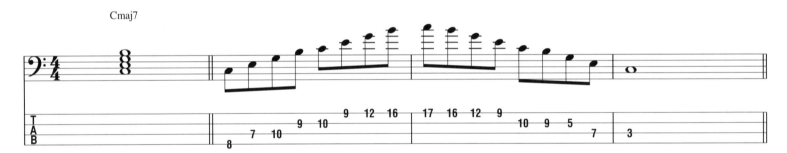

Minor seventh chords are built from the root, ♭3rd, 5th, and ♭7th (1–♭3–5–♭7) of the major scale, with the 3rd and 7th lowered a half step. They are written with any one the suffixes listed below.

	1	2	♭3	4	5	6	♭7	8
Cm7, Cmin7, C-7	C	D	E♭	F	G	A	B♭	C

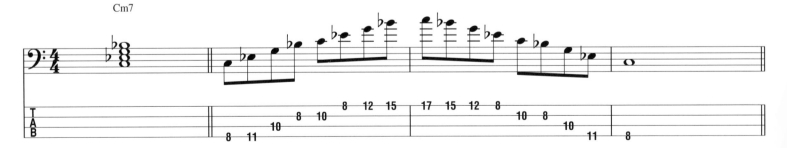

Dominant seventh chords are constructed from the root, 3rd, 5th, and ♭7th (1–3–5–♭7) of the major scale, with the 7th lowered a half step.

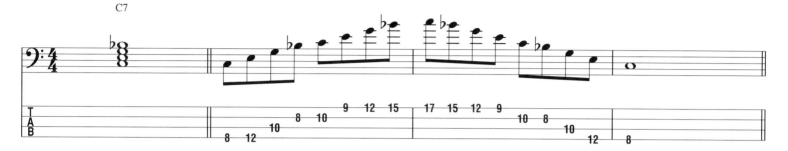

	1	2	3	4	5	6	♭7	8
C7	C	D	E	F	G	A	B♭	C

Now let's use some of these types of chords in a Technique Tune-Up…

TECHNIQUE TUNE-UP: FINGERING STRATEGIES

Playing any instrument requires intelligent fingering choices in order to economize the movement of our hands and fingers. However, we often reach a certain point in our fingering progress and plateau. Below are some basic ideas, reminders, and examples of clever or logical fingering choices that will hopefully help to inspire new ideas or work through problem areas.

The first reminder is that decisions on how to play a given passage are purely based on the *context* in which that passage appears. We should always ask ourselves: "Where is the note or phrase coming from and where is it headed?" For example, let's look at the various fingering choices listed below. Notice that the order of the fingers used changes substantially, depending on which notes precede and follow the four-note "cell."

Four-note cells:

Other examples:

* Roman numerals above show which string to play the note on.
(I = G string, II = D string, etc.)

For fast passages and multi-octave arpeggios, one clever option for making large position shifts is to use an open string in the phrase. Playing the open string gives us just enough extra time to make a big shift up or down the fingerboard and has the added benefits of being played with its full rhythmic note value and allowing a quick reference for our ears to ensure that we are playing in tune.

Here are some of the triads and seventh chords that we studied in the last section, played here with open strings. Notice that some are inverted, meaning a note other than the root is the lowest note of the chord.

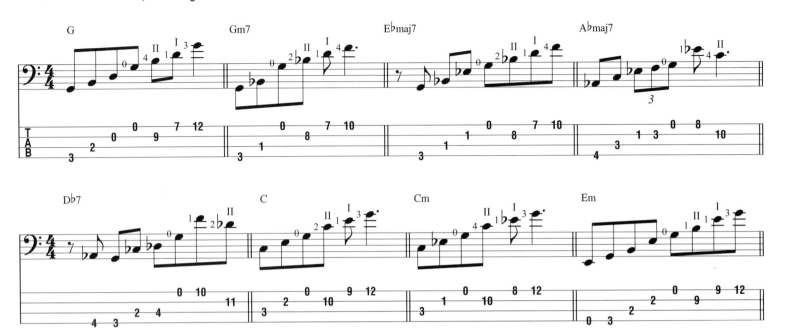

Most often, we are taught to play diatonic scales with three or more notes per string. While this allows for learning the fingerboard across the strings and accessing these notes within one position, it can box us in and create unnecessary or awkward shifts. We can become mentally "boxed in," as well, with less options quickly available to our fingers. Try to practice your scales with logical position shifts. This will expand your comfort with the neck and also provide the freedom to go various directions while improvising.

Here are some examples of the major scale that we learned but with alternate fingerings:

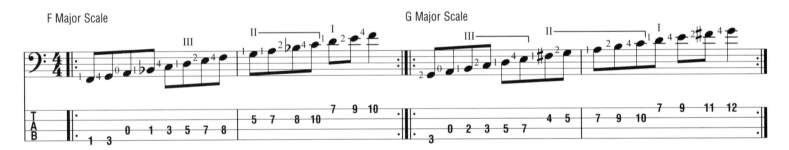

Now let's learn one of the most common chord progressions in jazz music…

CHANGES ARE INEVITABLE: THE ALL-IMPORTANT ii–V–I PROGRESSION

In Chapter 1, we discussed the V–I and IV–I cadences, as well as assigned Roman numerals to diatonic triads. Let's take this a bit further. Seventh chords use the same numerals as triads, but they almost always include suffixes (unlike triads).

Here are the diatonic seventh chords in the key of C major:

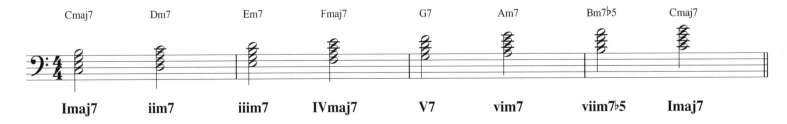

Remember that we also discussed how cadences, and specifically V–I, have the sound of resolving to the tonic. When we use the full dominant seventh chord for the V chord, the reason becomes clearer: there is a tritone built within the dominant seventh, and this dissonance (unstable sound) wants to resolve to consonance (stable sound). For instance, in a G7 chord, the intervallic distance from its 3rd to its ♭7th (B to F) is a diminished 5th. When moving to the I chord (Cmaj7), the B resolves a half step up to C, and the F resolves down to E.

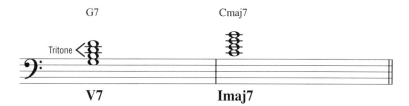

One of the most used and useful chord progressions in all of jazz harmony is the iim7–V7–Imaj7, commonly shortened to simply ii–V–I. Notice below that there are shared chord tones between the iim7 and V7 chords. The remaining chord tones sound good when played over the dominant chord itself.

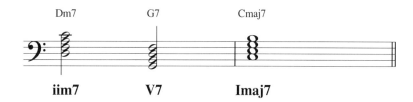

Because of this, musicians began to insert the iim7 before the V7 in order to create interest and color. By delaying the sound of the V7 chord, and providing more melodic possibilities, the movement of V–I became more pliable with the addition of the iim7.

Here are two other examples of the ii–V–I:

When in a minor key, or often when resolving to a minor chord, the ii–V–I has different chord qualities. The common shorthand for describing this cadence is "minor ii–V."

Let's apply our knowledge of the ii–V–I to the next section, where we'll learn to create bass lines.

BASS ACCOMPANIMENT: THE TWO-FEEL

Often the underdog of bass accompanying, the **two-feel** can be a powerful tool in how we arrange our bass lines, create dynamic rhythm, and manipulate musical tension and release. Early jazz tuba players began to morph a basic brass-band marching beat into a more syncopated and dance-like feel. Bassists, who sometimes were tuba players themselves, continued this primary rhythmic comping of two beats to a bar in a style similar to brass players. The crucial element to emphasize here is that the *rhythmic feel* is the first priority, with note choices an extremely close second.

Understanding how to build these note choices is a keystone in constructing all kinds of improvised bass lines, in any genre. Remember that the conventional function of the bass line is to clearly define the harmony, as well as to provide the foundation of that harmonic sound or color. This is generally achieved by playing the root of a given chord, usually on the downbeat, and utilizing chord tones in logical and clever ways that help to further define the harmony and provide support for the other melodies that occur simultaneously.

In the first examples below, you'll notice that the roots are played on the downbeats almost exclusively. And, as is common, the 5th of the chord is often chosen as the second note. Remember that the two-feel is based on the broad concept of playing two half notes per bar, adjusting the harmonic rhythm as necessary. So, if there are multiple chords within one bar, choosing the root is most often the preferred note.

It is fairly common for a rhythm section to play a two-feel during the head of a song and go to a walking bass line for solos (more on that later). Listening to great bassists like Arvell Shaw, Ray Brown, Oscar Pettiford, and Israel Crosby teaches us how best to play and use the two-feel concept.

In the exercise below, set your metronome to a medium tempo and mentally arrange the metronome sound so that you hear it as beats 2 and 4. Play these simple lines and focus on feeling each swung quarter note, even though you aren't playing them. You want to create as much forward motion and swing with basic half notes as you can.

Notice the minor ii–V in the second bar, and the ii–V–I that starts in bars 7–8 (Gm7–C7) and resolves to Fmaj7.

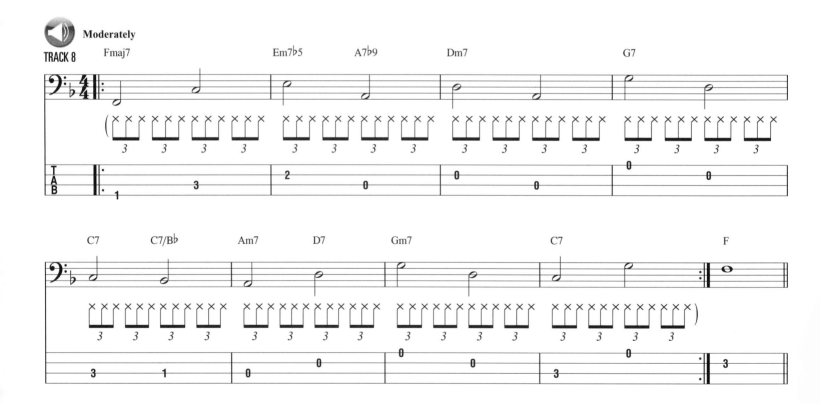

One way to maintain the sense of forward motion in your two-feel line is to place quarter notes in musical and logical parts of phrases.

Another very effective addition to the two-feel is a well-placed eighth note, where you help to fill out the swing feel. Best described in notation as the last note of an eighth-note triplet, this basic syncopation should move the feel forward to the next note. A common place to play this is on the "and" of beat 4.

Below is an example of a much more active two-feel. Notice, however, that all the extra notes ultimately serve to create a sense of movement, dance, and swing. See if you can identify all the ii-V or ii-V-I progressions in this one.

Here's an important point to keep in mind: the two-feel does not exist on a different rhythmic spectrum than a four-beats-per-bar walking line. Often, students will view the two-feel as separate from the feeling of walking, which may lead to a "soggy" rhythmic quality. Try to feel the undercurrent of polyrhythms that exist in the swing, and latch onto that sense of movement.

When transitioning from a two-feel to walking, there should be an impression of release from the "pent-up" energy of the underlying triplets, eighth notes, and quarter notes implied in your line.

Think about how you and your fellow rhythm-section team can use this simple concept in new and surprising ways. One of the great joys of this music is that we get to experiment together and discover new things every time that we play.

Next, we'll learn a new scale to use in our solo experimentations.

PREPARING TO SOLO: MINOR SCALES

In the last chapter, we discussed major and major pentatonic scales in certain keys. As you already know, a **key** is defined by the **tonic**—the note around which the key centers.

Below is a grouping of notes called the **natural minor scale**. Although the notes in the scale are the same as the key of Eb major, the tonic of the key is C, therefore the scale is C natural minor. When you look at the scale, examine the relationship and sequence of the intervals, using the tools we learned in Chapter 1.

C Natural Minor Scale

During the "common practice period" in classical music, composers were dissatisfied with the lack of tension in the **leading tone**, the seventh degree of the scale. For compositional movement, we need a sense of tension and release to create interest. So, the composers of that period altered the natural minor scale by raising the leading tone a half step, creating a new scale called the **harmonic minor scale**.

C Harmonic Minor Scale

But creating melodies with the harmonic minor was awkward because of the space between the sixth and seventh degrees of the scale. So, the composers added a second altered scale degree by also raising the sixth. The result was what we now call the **melodic minor scale**.

C Melodic Minor Scale

In classical music, there is a different pattern for ascending and descending the melodic minor scale, but let's use what's often called the "jazz minor" or "jazz melodic minor" pattern, which is simply the notes played the same in both directions.

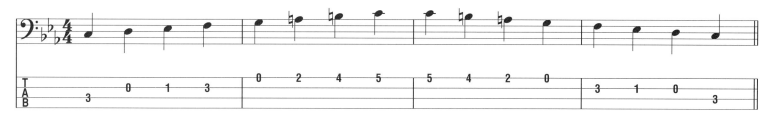

Lastly, remember the major pentatonic scale from Chapter 1? There is also a **minor pentatonic scale**, and we should learn it in all keys, too.

C Minor Pentatonic Scale

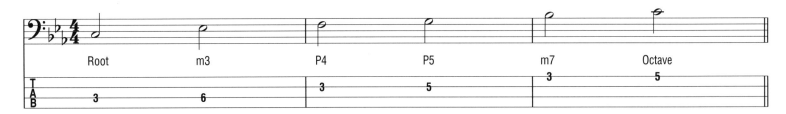

ALL EARS ON YOU: CREATING MELODIES OF YOUR OWN

Creating improvised melodies based on the main melodic theme of a song is a great place to start and a great tool to have available as a solo option. But another part of improvisation is creating new melodies of your own. How can we do this? First, play through the melody to the song "St. James Infirmary," shown below. Notice that it's created from the D natural minor scale.

SAINT JAMES INFIRMARY

Words and Music by Joe Primrose
Copyright © 2018 by HAL LEONARD LLC
International Copyright Secured   All Rights Reserved

As mentioned, we can use the melody as an effective springboard for our ideas. But what if we were just given the chord changes and were expected to improvise? We need to know not only what notes to play, but also what rhythms we can combine with these note choices.

In the following example, let's use the chord tones of the written changes and a rhythm of steady eighth notes. We can repeat chord tones where needed, and many times if we'd like to.

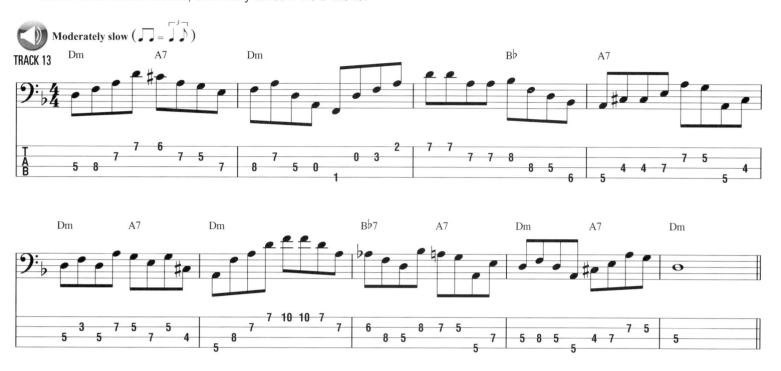

OK, we're on the right path, but this doesn't sound much like a solo yet. Let's try something else: use chord tones exclusively but mimic the *rhythm* of the main melody.

That should sound like a bit of an improvement to you. Hopefully, there's an interval, phrase, or note choice against a chord that you liked. Let's say, for example, that the simple rhythm in bar 2 grabbed your interest. Let's use just that rhythm across a section of the tune.

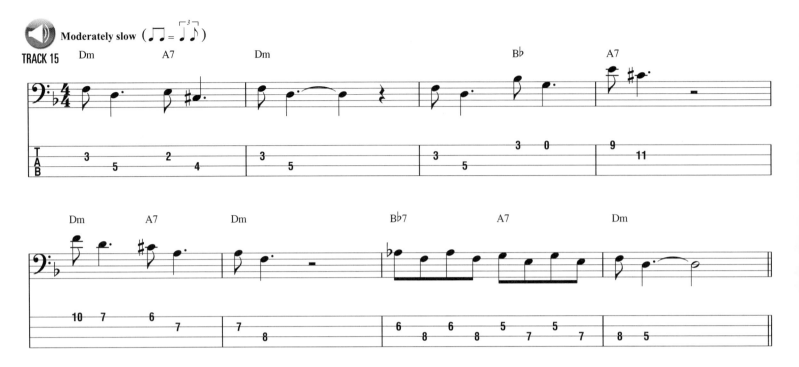

The next experiment might be to continue to use chord tones and that basic rhythm, but altering the intervals by changing their direction or octave, or by placing the rhythm in different parts of the measure.

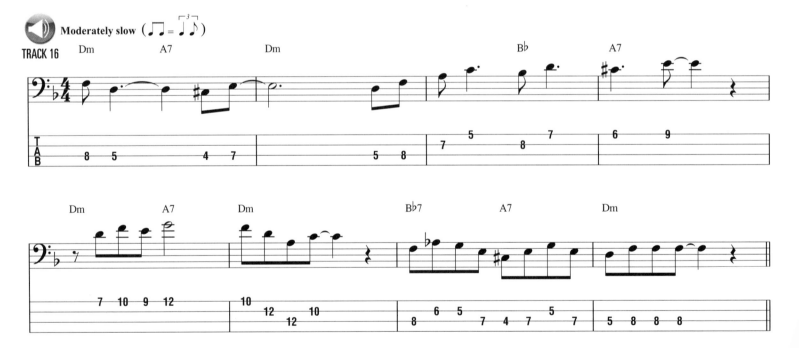

As you can see, there are boundless variations that you can create. While the note choices, phrasing, rhythms, and construction of the solo will get more diverse, the essential nature of the act remains constant: creating new melodies that fit with the existing harmony of the song. Use the play-a-long aspect of the recordings to explore some of your own ideas.

CHAPTER 3

LIVING IN HARMONY: CHORD EXTENSIONS

So far, we've explored the notes that create major, minor, and dominant seventh chords. These fundamental tones and their intervallic relationships define the quality of a given chord. But what about notes played in conjunction with a chord that aren't "chord tones"?

In this chapter, we begin to examine **extended chords**. Sometimes called "extensions" or just "tensions," these notes are part of the scale associated with a given chord; specifically, they are the second, fourth, and sixth scale degrees.

Because they are usually "voiced" above the root's octave, we add 7 to their original scale degree to indicate that they are played above the chord tones. The result are tensions called the **9th** (2 + 7), **11th** (4 + 7), and **13th** (6 + 7).

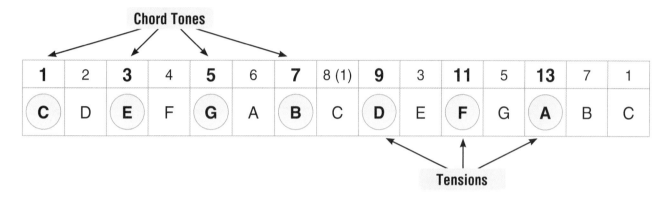

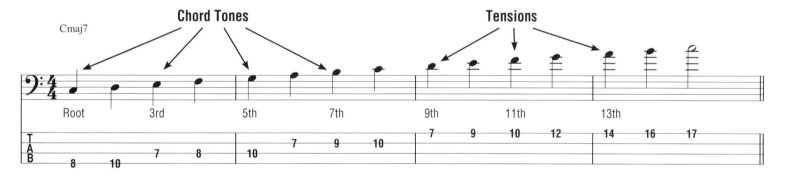

While these tensions are technically available to play at any given time, they aren't necessarily all played together. In fact, certain tensions are generally avoided with certain chord qualities because of a particular dissonance or confusion of the intended sound.

A common example would be a major 9th chord, written "maj9." This means that the composer intends for the extension of the 9th to be played as part of the chord's voicing. The fact that only the "9" is written *implies* that the 7th is also present in the chord. And by seeing the quality, "major," we know that the 7th is natural.

Cmaj9

	1	2	3	4	5	6	7	8 (1)	9
Cmaj9	C	D	E	F	G	A	B	C	D

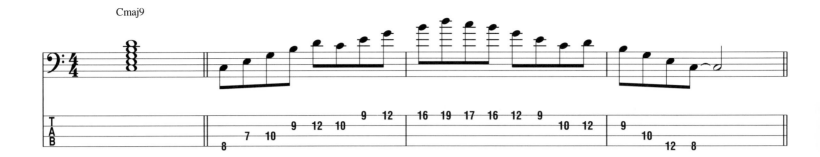

Cmaj9

If you see a root with an extension but no chord quality (C9, C13, etc.), this means that the chord quality is dominant. So, a "C9" would be a C7 with the 9th added.

	1	2	**3**	4	**5**	6	**♭7**	8 (1)	**9**
C9	C	D	E	F	G	A	B♭	C	D

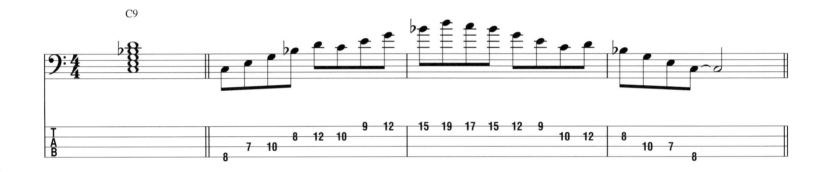

C9

A common example that uses the 11th extension is a minor 11th, where the tension works well with the chord makeup.

	1	2	**♭3**	4	**5**	6	**♭7**	8 (1)	9	♭3	**11**
Cm11	C	D	E♭	F	G	A	B♭	C	D	E♭	F

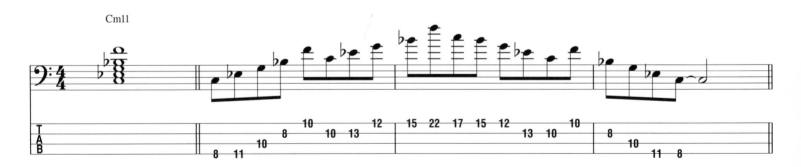

Cm11

We'll look at extended chords and altered tensions more extensively as we progress through the chapters. For now, let's use some of these extended chords in our next Technique Tune-Up.

TECHNIQUE TUNE-UP: SWING TIME

Pocket, groove, hump, swing, tip—all of these are words associated with the rhythmic attitude in straight-ahead jazz. This elusive, sometimes controversial, and nearly-impossible-to-notate feeling is part of what makes jazz so great.

Because this music is both oral and aural, it's critically important to listen to great players to absorb and replicate the swing feeling. There are no books, technical devices, or apps that will teach us; recordings and live performances are the source, period.

All that said, it is helpful to be able to use the written word and musical notation to try and further communicate ideas. In that spirit, let's look a bit more closely at the most often used notation device to try and encapsulate swung eighth notes.

First, let's examine how the triplet undercurrent can be felt in the swing feel. Rather than assigning the word "tri-pl-et" to count along with the figure, we see the syllables "doo-dle-la." Repeat the "doo-dle-la" syllables in time and then slightly shift the emphasis to the "la" syllable. This starts the feeling of a pronounced upbeat, which is crucial to swing.

Next in the example, we've changed the notation to quarter/eighth groupings to further demonstrate the idea. The "dle" syllable is silent or sounded in the throat rather than pronounced. Add slightly more emphasis on the "la" syllable. You should start to hear what sounds like shuffled, or swung, eighth notes.

Finally, we wrap up the example by demonstrating how we might see this notation written and how the earlier parts of the exercise can be applied to conventional notation.

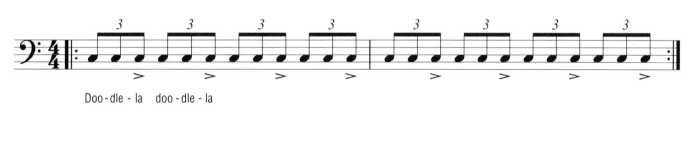

Doo - dle - la   doo - dle - la

Doo (dle) la   doo(dle) la

Written rhythm

Felt rhythm

Walking bass lines are the "meat and potatoes" of a bass player's job. Below is an example of a walking line in which the triplet undertone is clearly heard in the eighth notes. It also represents the notation and extended chords that we discussed earlier. Notice that we're not required to play every note of an extended chord. Although the first chord is D9, we are fine sticking close to a basic dominant seventh chord construction (1–3–5–♭7). Usually the chordal or solo instrument will cover the tension.

One clever idea that I learned from an instructor of mine was to think of all the quarter notes in a walking line as beat 1. What this means is that you consider each note to have the same intensity and forward motion that we usually reserve for beat 1 of each new measure. The effect is understated but noticeable.

Pay attention to the extended chords in bars 7–9, 12, 14, and 16.

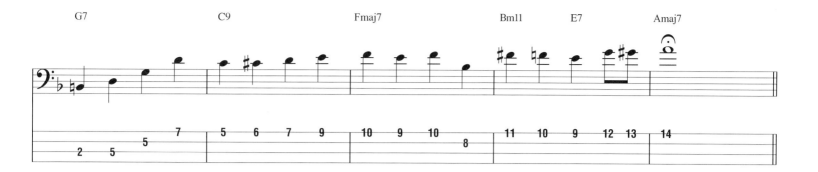

Below is an example that dispels the myth about repeating bass lines and demonstrates "laying in the pocket." Notice that there are only a few eighth-note skips and very little ornamentation. Also, each chord is a minor 9th. The emphasis is on the relaxed intensity of driving the band with the time-feel, rather than choosing "hip" notes just to impress.

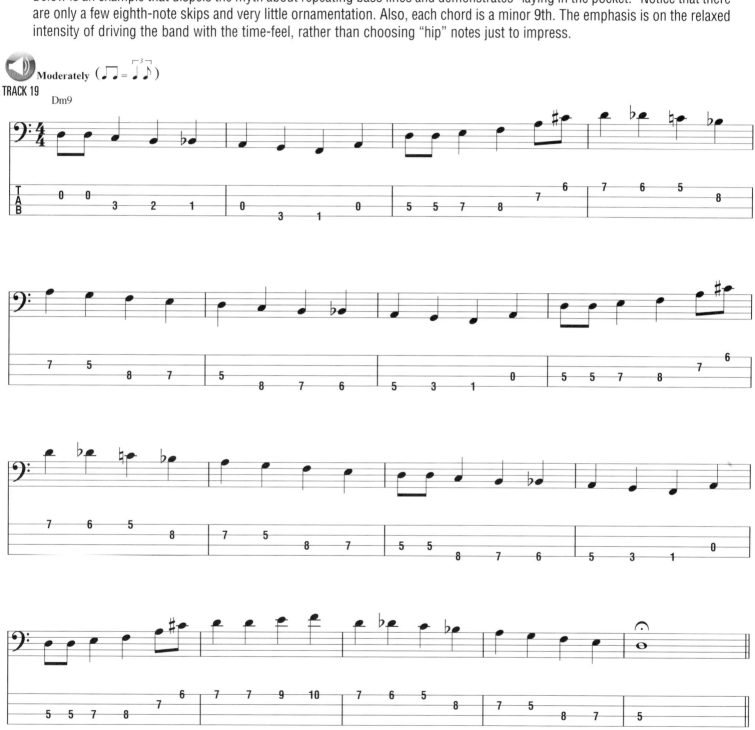

To summarize, when trying to "tip," we're looking for a loping, lilting, lifting sense of forward motion. The feeling is simultaneously grounded and light and contains both triple and duple meter.

CHANGES ARE INEVITABLE: THE I–vi–ii–V PROGRESSION

In Chapter 2, we explored the ubiquitous ii–V–I progression. Expanding on that, there is another commonly used progression that appears often, the Imaj7–vim7–iim7–V7 (usually shortened to "I–vi–ii–V"), which furthers the idea of delay and resolution.

The Imaj7 is the key center and often called the tonic chord. Examining the vim7, you'll notice that it shares some common notes with the Imaj7. Because of this, we also consider the vim7 to be a tonic chord.

Like the previously mentioned delaying of the V7 chord, the vim7 extends the sound of the tonic. It adds slightly different colors to the sound palate, but maintains the same basic harmonic function.

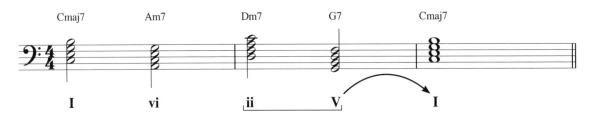

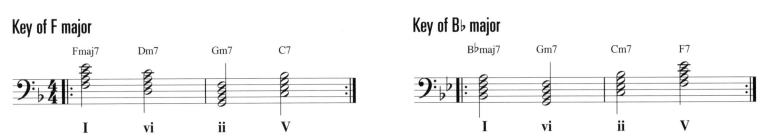

Note: You will often see the chord quality of the vim7 written as a dominant seventh instead. Just by changing the minor 3rd in the minor chord to a major 3rd, a whole new sound opens up. This is logical use of the dominant chord quality since the dominant quality wants to resolve to the root of its relative tonic chord—in this case, the root of the next chord, iim7.

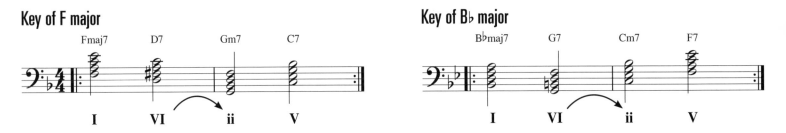

Additionally, a conventional way to abstract or extend the sound of a key center even further is to use the iiim7, which is also a close relative of the Imaj7.

So, the I–vi–ii–V is often altered to iii–vi–ii–V, with the first two chords still representing the key center. These are subtleties that help to give this music such elegance.

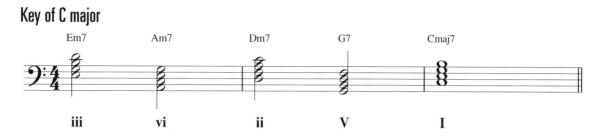

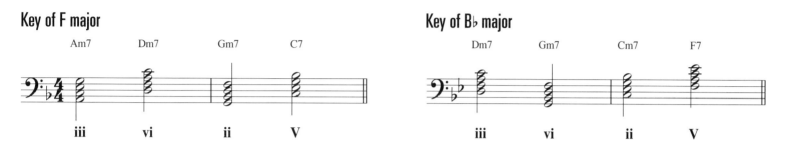

We're going to use these two common progressions to dive deeply into the next section on the critical walking bass line.

BASS ACCOMPANIMENT: WALKING BASS LINES

A staple of jazz bass, the walking bass line has come to help define conventional jazz as we know it. The walking bass line grew from the "oom-pah" beat of the marching-band tuba. Early New Orleans musicians, seeking a more fluid rhythmic accompaniment than the big brass instrument, found a more pleasing blend with the double bass. Additionally, because the instrument doesn't directly involve a breath, a string of unbroken notes could lay the foundation for the melodies on top. Master musicians turned this simple concept into something truly great.

Unfortunately, there are no real shortcuts to greatness. Because the commitment to mastery is such a long-term one, it's important to clearly define our goals as we strive to be virtuosos in our craft.

The walking bass line provides a rhythmic and harmonic foundation that helps to "glue" the performance together. By reinforcing the chord changes with a firm rhythmic drive, the walking line affords the other ensemble members a secure "pad" on which to improvise.

Many of the characteristics of a good bass line are directly in line with what we may view as qualities of great music in general. When we apply them directly to our bass line accompaniment, they can become specific signposts for assessing the music that we are creating. Clearly, our most important goal should be to make good music, regardless of our instrument.

The following list covers some of the elements that make up a great bass line in the tradition of Paul Chambers, Arvell Shaw, Ray Brown, Oscar Pettiford, Charles Mingus, Wilbur Ware, and the many other exceptional bass players of yesterday and today.

A good bass line should have:

- Good sound
- Accurate intonation
- Good feeling for listeners and the ensemble
- Rhythmic accuracy and control
- Swing with forward motion and buoyancy
- Support for the ensemble and soloist
- Harmonic awareness and accuracy

- Relentlessness, confidence, and strength
- Cogent melodies
- Appropriate dynamics
- Variation in rhythm, melody, and harmony
- Connections, even abstract, to the song's root melody and harmony

Aspects of musical basics, swing feel, technique, and performance basics are in this list, and our bass lines should naturally reflect them. So, it's incumbent upon us to examine, assimilate, and manipulate a wide range of rhythmic, melodic, and harmonic aspects of the language. By studying the lineage of the master musicians who came before us, we can understand and utilize concepts of musical logic and dynamism. Sam Jones, Ron Carter, Israel Crosby, Jimmie Blanton, Walter Page, Milt Hinton, Scott LaFaro, Jimmy Garrison, Slam Stewart, and Red Mitchell are just some of the names for us to study and emulate.

We need to create sonic "signposts" for the listener and our bandmates to keep the song cohesive. By choosing logical notes on the strong beats of a bar (1 and 3 in 4/4 time), we can help to center the harmony of the moment, as well as the harmonic rhythm of the whole piece.

Generally speaking, every time there is a chord change, the root of the new chord is played on the downbeat. This is not a hard-and-fast rule per se, but it is a great place to start and will be a signpost that listeners are expecting.

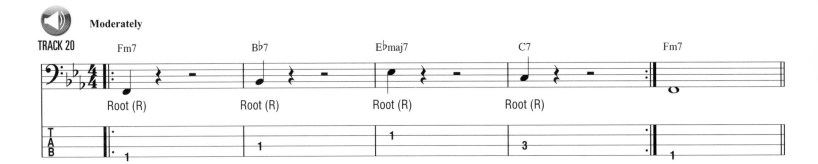

So, this gives us beat 1, but what about the other three beats in a measure of 4/4? This is where we begin to craft our own sound. Let's begin by clearly outlining the harmony in each measure with root notes and root octaves.

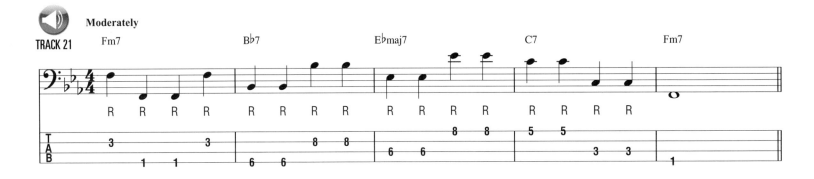

Here, we introduce 3rds:

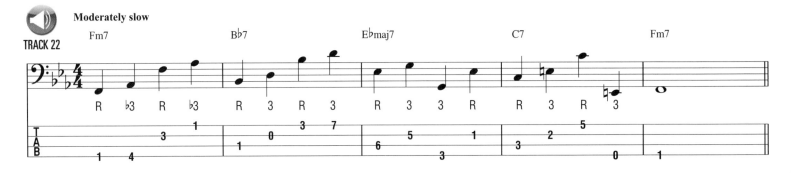

And now 5ths:

TRACK 23

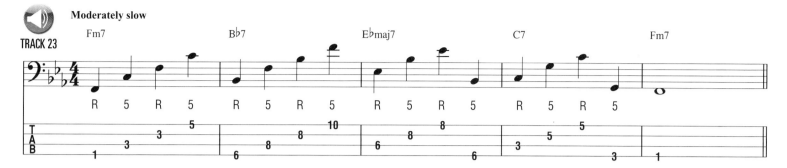

The next chord tone to focus on is the 7th:

TRACK 24

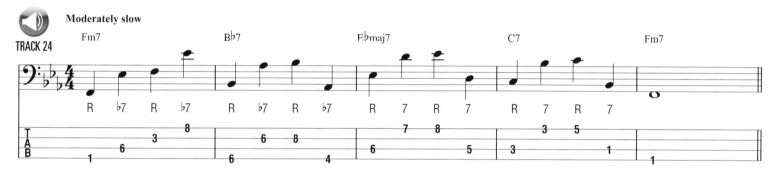

Now let's combine the octaves, 3rds, and 5ths. At this stage, we're using basic triads.

TRACK 25

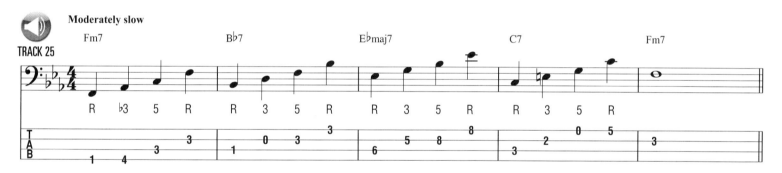

By including the 7ths, we add a great color to the sound. And by beginning to change the direction of the lines, we introduce greater variety to the music.

TRACK 26

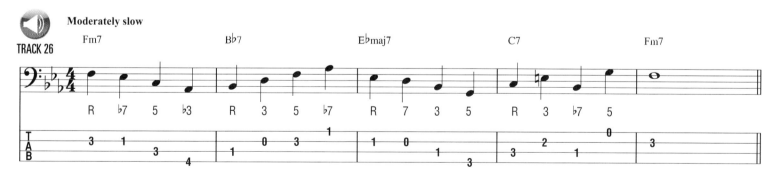

So far, we've played the root of the chord on each bar's downbeat. As previously mentioned, this is extremely common, but it's not an unbreakable rule by any means, as demonstrated below.

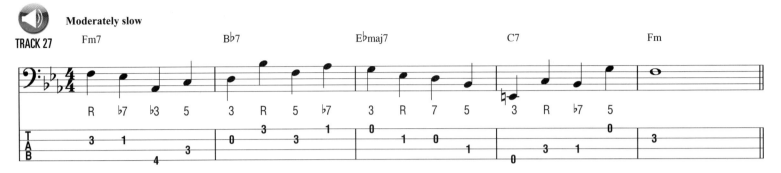

So much music already, and we've only used chord tones! In our next section on soloing, we'll take a look at the modes that we can use for more note options.

PREPARING TO SOLO: MODES

As we learn scales, it's important not to stay fixated on one way of playing them. There are several ways that you can play with the structure of a scale for musical goals.

One way that you can manipulate scales is by arranging the notes into modes. For example, you could play the notes of the E♭ major scale in order, but start and end on the note F. The result is the F Dorian mode.

While modes are part of a "parent" scale, they are considered unique scales in and of themselves. Below are the modes of the major scale: Ionian, Dorian, Phrygian, Lydian, Mixolydian, Aeolian, and Locrian. Remember: these are still the notes of the E♭ major scale, just starting and ending on different notes.

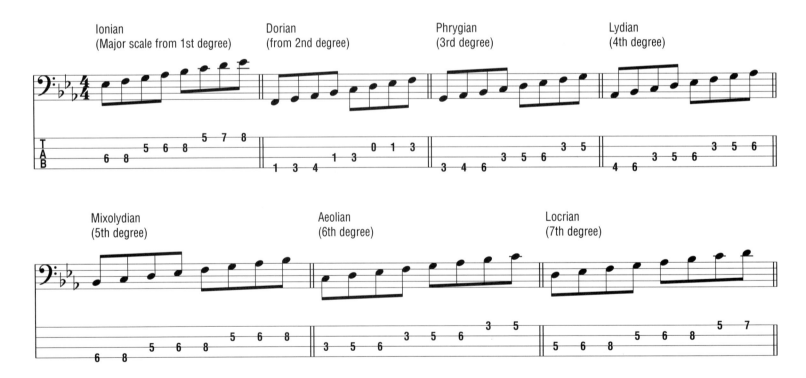

Now let's learn how to use these modes in both walking bass lines and solos…

ALL EARS ON YOU, PART 1: CONNECTING NOTES

Movement is a word that covers many different aspects of a successful walking bass line or solo phrase. Rhythmic movement, melodic movement, forward movement, movement in progressing from one note to another… There are many ways to achieve the movement that we're after.

Consider the following ways that one note can move to another, focusing first on walking bass lines:

Stepwise scalar movement means that the note we choose in between two notes remains in the same range as the target note. We can use a variety of scales to choose from, but the idea remains consistent: that we approach the target note from below or above, using the closest note from the appropriate scale. Here are some sample bass lines played over the chords from our first walking bass line. Each example has a chosen chord scale written out to clue you in on note choices.

F Dorian Scale

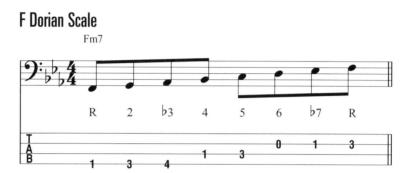

This B♭ connects the A♭ and C. It is stepwise movement between the two notes using the F Dorian scale. The C is the "target" note.

B♭ Mixolydian Scale

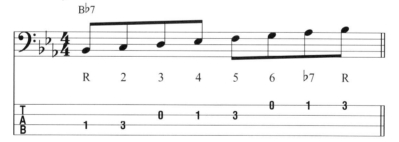

This G approaches the F with stepwise movement using the B♭ Mixolydian scale.

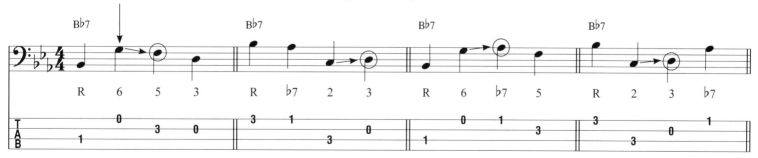

E♭ Ionian Scale

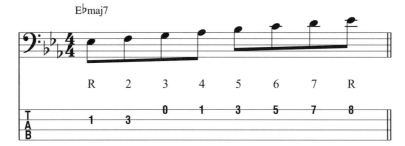

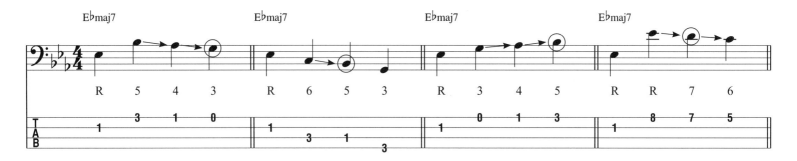

Chromatic movement refers to how we can approach a note from above or below, but specifically with a half step. Of course, there are many half-step approaches in many different kinds of scales, but with chromatic-approach movement, we are focusing on the technique of arriving at the target note by way of a minor 2nd above or below, regardless of what that chromatic note "means" to a given scale.

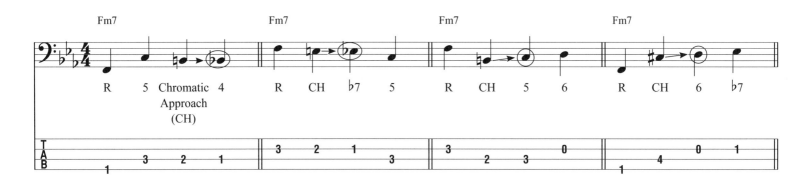

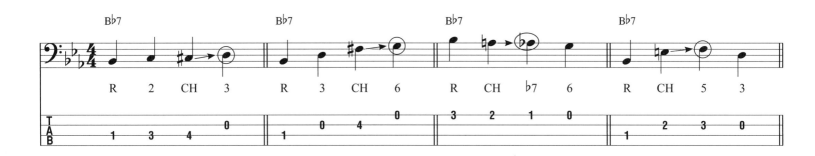

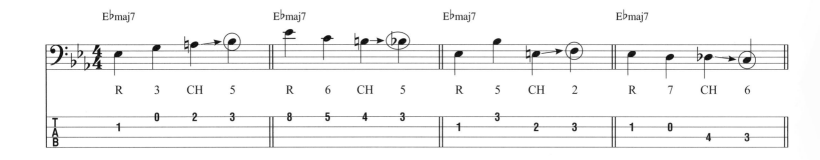

Approaching a target note by an interval larger than a major or minor 2nd is generally considered a **leap**. The bass line—or, more appropriately, bass line *melody*—will stick out a bit if it incorporates leaping approaches, but they can be used to great effect. Approaching a note by a leap without a musical context or reason can make the line sound disjointed or unfocused, so be sure to use this technique carefully.

Let's summarize where we are so far in terms of creating our own bass line: By clearly providing strong harmonic signposts that connect in logical and interesting ways, we are creating melodies with our bass line that have style and function.

Below is a sample bass line that combines all these concepts. Can you find the different kinds of movement we've discussed?

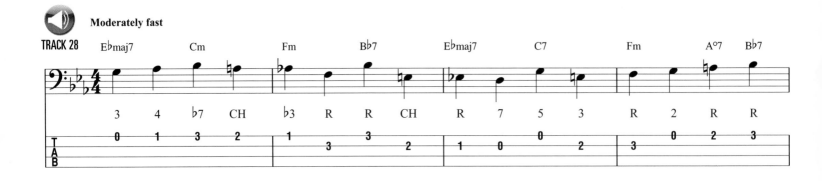

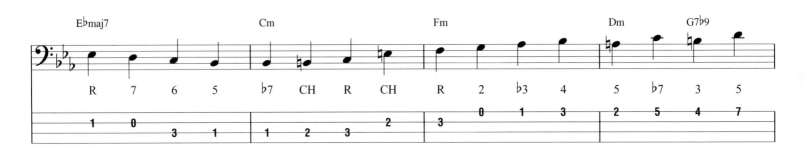

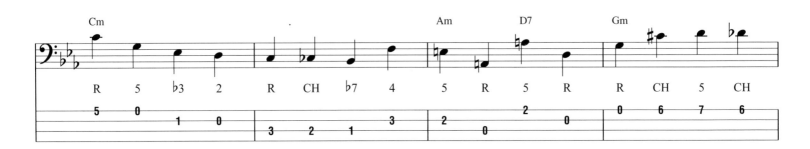

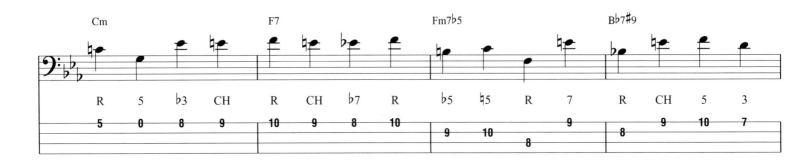

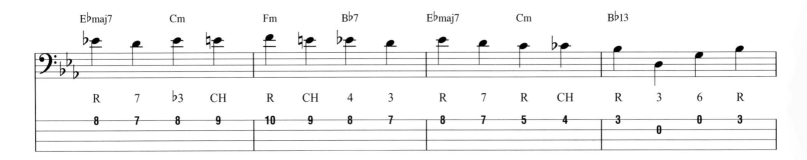

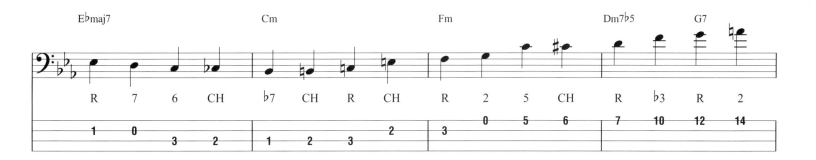

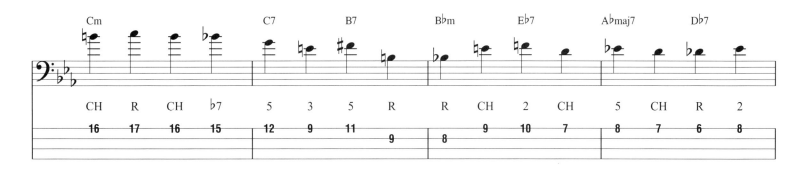

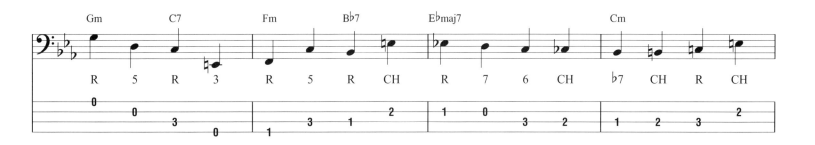

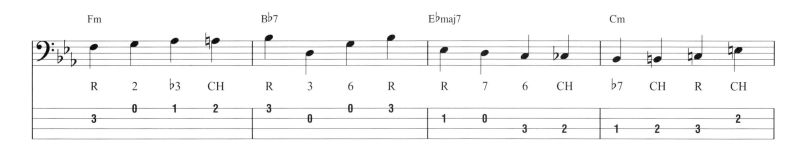

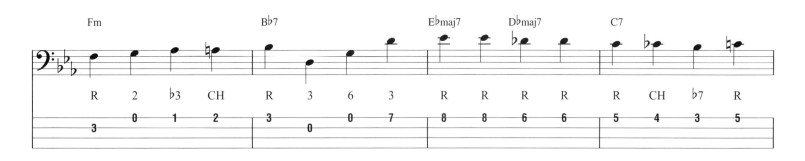

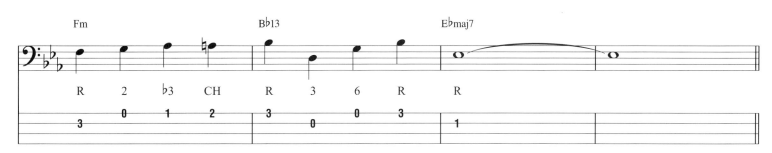

By examining each note of a bass line in context, we can find examples of techniques that we can use to build our own. And with the wide range of note choices, approaches, rhythms, and registers, there's nearly a limitless amount of possibilities for creating good lines.

I would be remiss, however, if I didn't mention that we need to maintain some perspective about these lines that we are creating. Keep in mind that all this analysis of scales and numbers is secondary to the greater purpose of making good music overall. The harmonic options that we discussed earlier are just symbols on paper that represent a much richer palette of colors of sound. The movement between two given notes is still part of a larger melody. And all of our own playing usually is created in tandem with other musicians who we need to support and respond to.

Here's an anecdote to illustrate my point: The great bassist George "Pops" Foster, who is credited with being one of the first innovators of how the bass is used in jazz, was asked how he chose the notes in his bass lines. He's said to have replied: "I just play any ol' go-to-hell note!"

While the specific words might not be the best direction for playing, the spirit of being so engaged in the music that the notes are secondary is a worthwhile attitude to adopt. Since we shouldn't actually ignore our note choices, let's continue to look at tools for choosing notes for soloing.

ALL EARS ON YOU, PART 2: CHORD SCALES

So far, we've learned a few scales and seen how a scale might connect to a chord, and vice versa. As we dig deeper into the idea of improvisational soloing, let's take a closer look at where our note choices can come from.

The term **chord scale** broadly refers to the application of certain scale options while a particular chord is being played. Generally, there are multiple scales, or versions of scales, that can apply to a single chord change, and so the term "chord scale" alludes to the various groups of notes that you can choose to create new melodies.

At its most foundational level, a chord scale is just a way to communicate various sounds at any given moment within your bass line or solo. As mentioned earlier, there is a "color," or harmonic palette, that is created when chord progressions are played. We just want to have many options of complimentary notes available for those colors.

A very basic example would be the modes of the major scale and the progression we studied earlier, the I–vi–ii–V. If all of these chord qualities are perfectly diatonic to the key of Eb, we can choose the appropriate mode for each root of the chord.

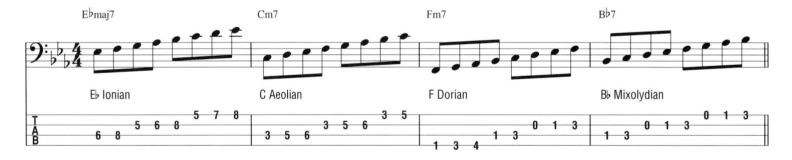

What's neat about chord scales is that we're not bound by the root of the chord itself. Remember: the idea is to find notes that "work" with the chord. A basic example would be to apply one of the modes to one of the other chords, given that the notes will fit. Here are a few samples:

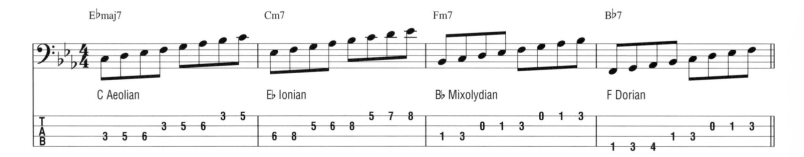

48

But what if a chord in a progression isn't diatonic? For example, earlier we saw Imaj7–VI7–iim7–V7. In this instance, we need to, first and foremost, respect the chord tones. So, for the C7, our chord scale choices must include an E natural, the 3rd of the C dominant seventh chord. The presence of the ♮3rd (E) and ♭7th (B♭) matches the C Mixolydian mode almost perfectly. For now, the rest of the notes of the scale should match the key signature—in this case, E♭ major: C–D–E♭–F–G–A♭–B♭.

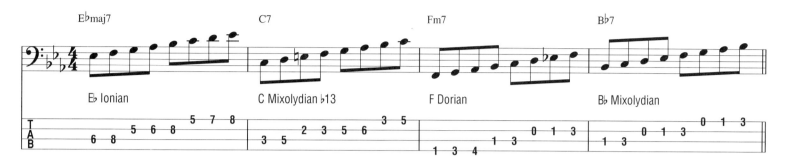

We've seen natural and flat 3rds and 7ths before, but what about this A♭? In this instance, it would be called a ♭13th, one of a handful of chord tensions that we'll look closely at in the coming chapters. The ♭13th is the perfect note choice for this progression because it inherently falls within the key of E♭ major, but a plain Mixolydian mode with an A natural would also work well here.

Lastly, it's important to understand that using modes is just a simple example. There are many, many kinds of scales that we can apply in many ways. Another simple example is the use of the major pentatonic scales that we learned about in Chapter 1. Look at how many different pentatonic scales fit our I–vi–ii–V progression:

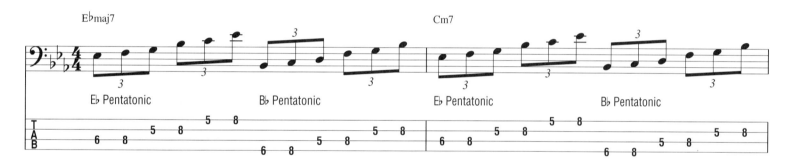

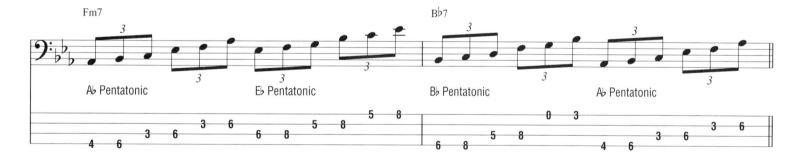

Remember, too, that, like our walking bass line notes, the melody is our main focus. There have been countless examples of master musicians playing notes that shouldn't "work" according to chord scales or analysis, but, because of the context and the melody, they are perfect. Keep this in mind as you use chord scales while building a solo.

As before, we'll use everything from this chapter about extended chords, walking bass lines, and connecting notes as we continue to build our foundation of playing in Chapter 4.

CHAPTER 4

LIVING IN HARMONY: MAJOR AND MINOR 6THS AND SUSPENDED CHORDS

There are more four-note chords for us to learn, and I find them pretty interesting, partially because some aren't used very often, but they have a great sound.

The first one is the **major sixth chord**. This is just like a major seventh chord, but the 6th replaces the 7th. It can substitute for a major seventh chord in many song situations.

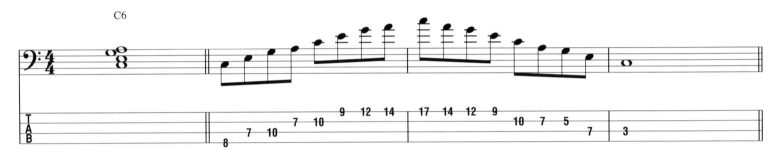

And next, as you might guess, is the **minor sixth chord**. This is just like a minor seventh chord, with the 6th replacing the 7th. This chord can often be used to substitute for a minor seventh chord but should be done carefully so as not to clash with the key of the chord progression.

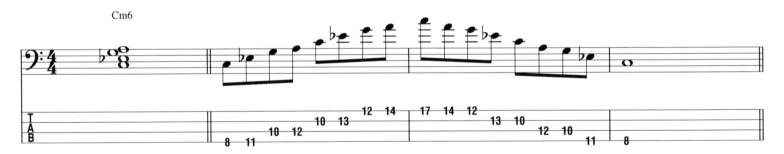

A **dominant seventh suspended chord** (sus4) is so-called because the sound is neither major nor minor. The fourth degree of the scale replaces the 3rd. Often used to substitute for or precede a dominant seventh, the dominant seventh sus4 chord is very versatile.

	1	2	3	4	5	6	♭7	8
C7sus4	C	D	E	F	G	A	B♭	C

So far, we've seen major and minor triads, seventh, and sixth chords, as well as augmented and diminished triads, suspended seventh, and dominant seventh chords. Keep practicing all of these and remember them as we move on.

TECHNIQUE TUNE-UP: SKIPPING

The technique called **skipping** can be a handy tool in adding interest to a bass line. As the name implies, the effect focuses on the *feeling* of the rhythm, like you might have felt as a child when you skipped down the street.

It's a simple concept that can be used to significant effect. Be careful, however, not to overdo it. Too much skipping, and you'll fall! But, seriously, it's easy to lose the grounded feeling of the time if the technique is used too often within a song.

The basic idea of a skip is just that: we add a well-placed eighth note in a walking line to propel the rhythm forward or to give it some extra life where needed.

Here's a sample walking bass line that uses major sixth, suspended seventh, and dominant seventh chords, played first without skips and then with skips:

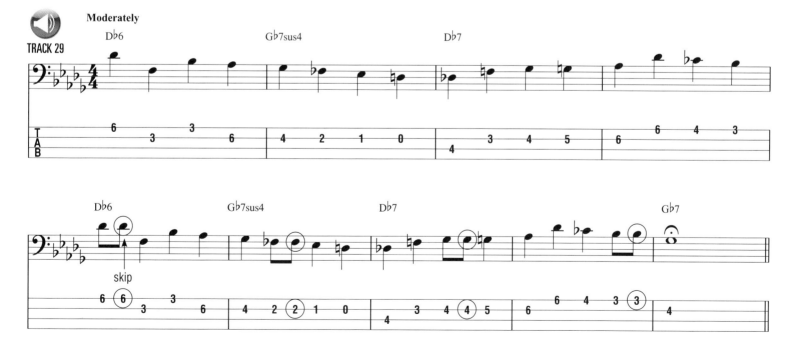

Because of the ergonomics of the bass, it's fairly common to use an open string as your skip note:

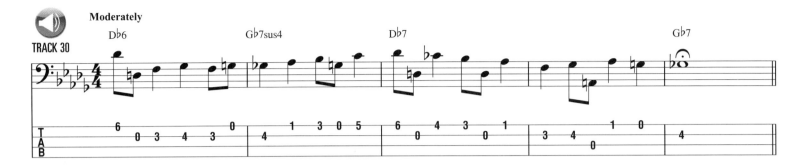

Another variation of the skip is to make the eighth note a muted, percussive sound instead of a clearly heard pitch. So, for example, you might pluck the open D string, but your fretting hand won't actually be pressing down on a note. The fretting hand does, however, rest against the open string, causing a percussive sound that can be used to the same effect as a skip with a fretted note.

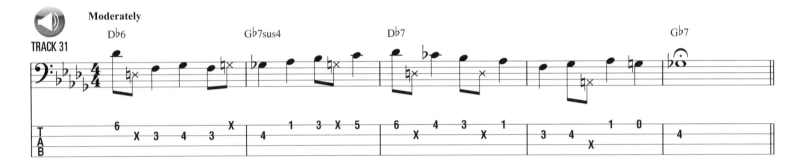

CHANGES ARE INEVITABLE: THE BLUES PROGRESSION

Created by African slaves brought to North America in the 18th and 19th centuries, the music we call the **blues** has had a monumental impact on jazz and all other music that followed.

The "blues" implies many things and has many meanings, but let's examine the chord progression that was codified over time and is most commonly played in jazz situations.

In its most fundamental construction, the blues progression contains only the I, IV, and V chords and in a particular pattern. Early blues chords were often the major-sixth sounds we discussed earlier, as in the traditional blues example shown below.

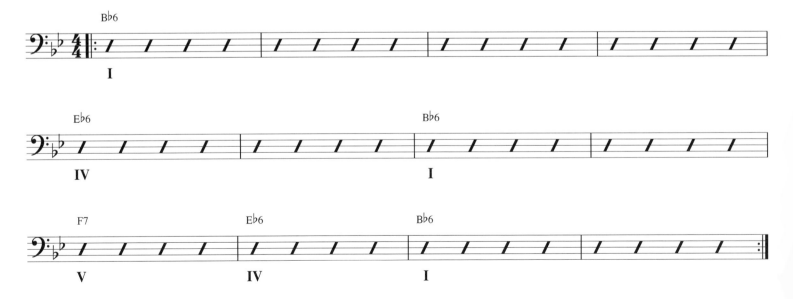

There are many, many variations on this format, but, in general, a conventional blues has 12 bars and the standard sequence of chords just shown.

Jazz musicians, in an effort to seek out more melodic and harmonic possibilities, systematized a few tweaks to this core progression, as shown below. Notice the differences in measures 2 and 9–12 and that the major sixth chords evolved into dominant seventh chords.

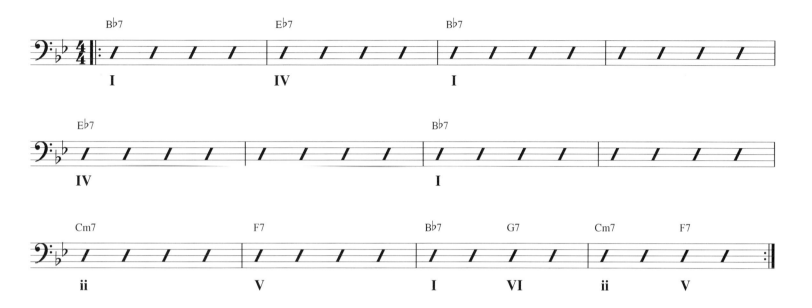

Below are a few more widely used additions and alterations to the progression. The basic structure, I–IV–V–IV–I, remains the same, but with further embellishment.

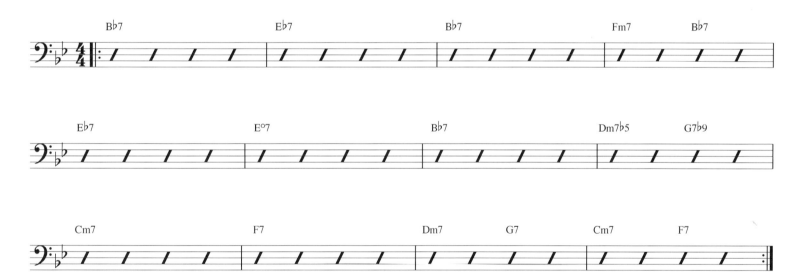

As you have noticed, the I and IV chords are dominant seventh in quality as opposed to major seventh. With their nearly limitless options, using dominant chords here provides a broad melodic palette on which to improvise. In this context, we don't think of the dominant chords by their *function*, but by their overall sound and ability to accept a wide variety of melodic ideas.

In the next section, we'll use the typical blues form to investigate some different ways to create walking bass lines and solos. Because of its common use, ease of understanding, and ability to be shaped and molded, the blues form is a great vehicle for exploring many musical concepts.

BASS ACCOMPANIMENT: THE SHAPE OF LINES TO COME

We've learned about the basics of how to create a walking bass line, so now let's venture into a broader, more musical perspective than simply moving from chord change to chord change.

Wide stretches of a walking bass line generally fall into one of these four categories: *linear, angular, landscape,* or *two-tiered.* It's important to be thinking of our lines in bigger portions rather than just the bar of the moment. In that regard, it's helpful to study the visual notation of the bass lines of great players. This gives us clues as to how they approached the music from a more macro level. Additionally, placing the shape of the bass line in the context of the music that is surrounding it is an interesting exercise. You may find that angular lines match a soloist's fervor, or perhaps a smooth landscape might be a counterpoint to that same solo intensity.

Linear lines are phrases that strongly favor continuous progress in a specific direction over multiple measures.

Here is an example of an ascending linear line in an F blues progression:

And here is a descending linear example played over another blues chord progression:

Angular lines can have either multiple measures of intervals that vary in direction, or a whole phrase that "jumps around" more than a linear bass line.

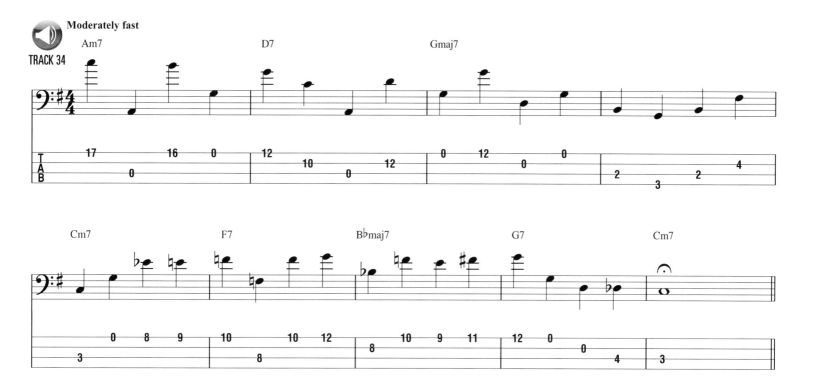

Landscape lines form a visual sense of continuous but varied up and down movement. It's as if the notes graphically represent hills in the distance. Below is an example played over the blues form that we learned. Notice how the alternating direction of the lines simulates a range of hills, and that the downbeats of measures 2, 4, 6–8, and 10–12 are not roots, but other chord tones.

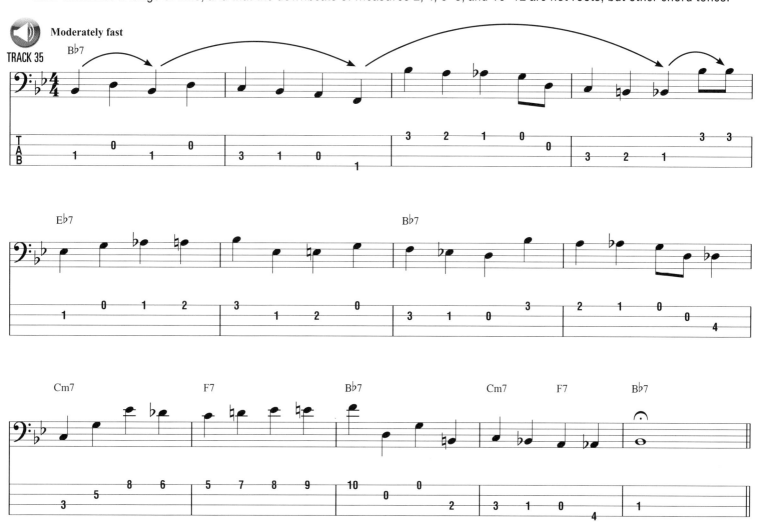

Two-tiered lines could also be considered "call-and-response" bass lines. They are also angular, but create the illusion of two separate lines occurring side by side. Below are the first eight bars of a blues in the key of G. Bars 5, 6, and 8 don't feature roots on the downbeats of the measures.

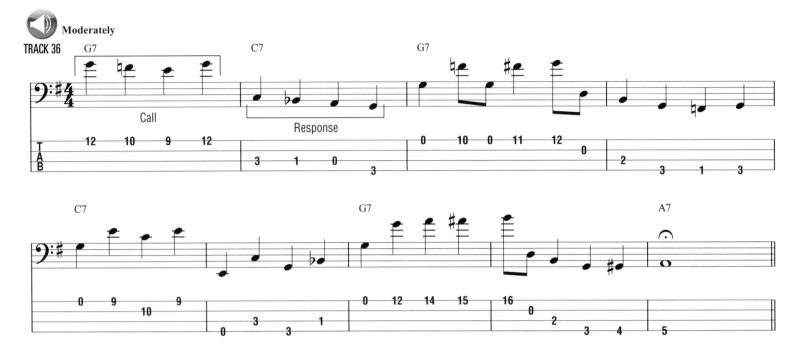

PREPARING TO SOLO: THE BLUES SCALE

In Chapter 3 we were introduced to the concept of chord scales and how they allow us to organize sounds that function in different ways against certain harmony. Now let's begin gathering a variety of chord scales that are more independent from key centers, scales that will apply more specifically to a single type of chord or will create a single kind of sound.

For example, the **blues scale** has some unique qualities that distinguish it from modes or pentatonic scales, which we learned about earlier.

When we construct the blues scale in its most rudimentary form, the scale is made up of six notes that can be thought of, if helpful, as a pentatonic scale with an extra note. Like other scales, there is a distinction between a major blues scale and a minor blues scale.

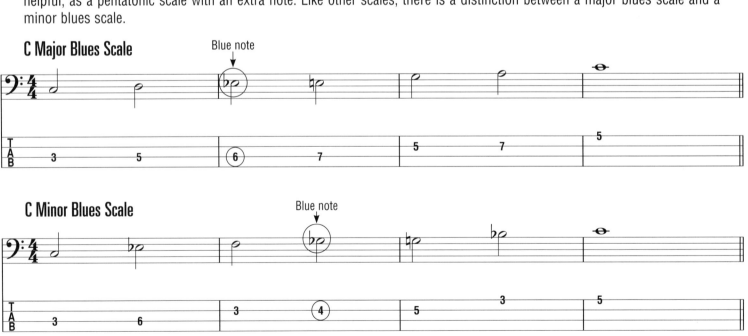

What is important to note about all of these ways of viewing or creating a blues scale is that each one includes what are often called **blue notes**: the ♭3rd and ♭5th. The juxtaposition of these notes against the chord tones (the ♮3rd and ♮5th), creates an organic dissonance that alludes to both African scales and the vocal "moans" of blues singing.

ALL EARS ON YOU: COMPOSITION IN REAL TIME

Now that we've learned about the form, scale, and progression, how might we approach soloing over the blues? First, let's lay the basic seven-note blues scale over the form, with a variety of rhythmic patterns, just to explore some options.

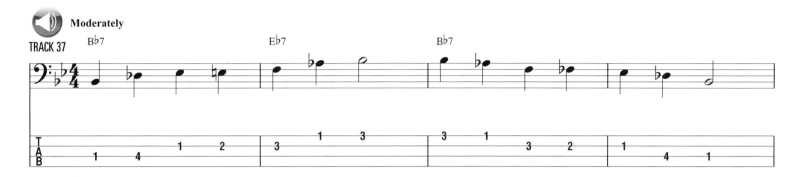

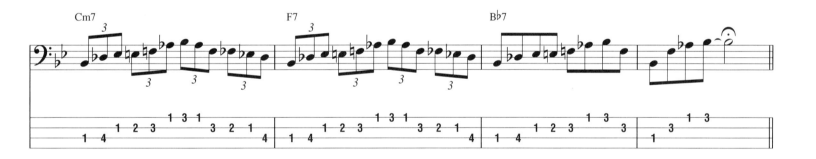

Now, using just the notes from this scale, let's create a simple solo chorus.

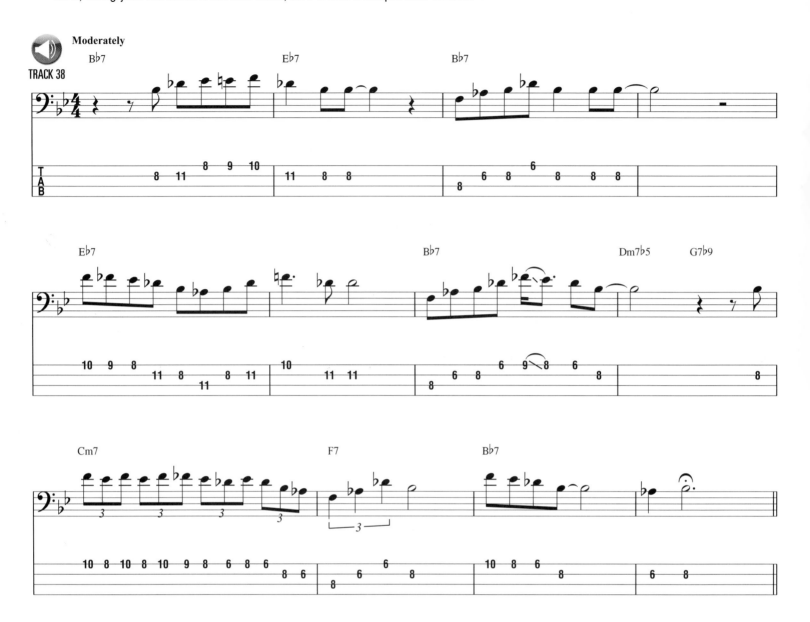

Notice that the principles we've already discussed still apply, though we're using this new "tool," the blues scale. We can think of improvising as "composition in the moment," and like typical composition, we have a huge variety of other tools at our disposal.

Perhaps you'd like to set up a bit of an unconventional option and "trade" with the drums. In which case, you would exchange solo phrases with the drummer. Let's use the blues scale in our portions of the trading:

We might, for example, choose to essentially make our solo a walking bass line. This would be a good time to internally hear and then execute your best walking skills.

As a beginning composer/improviser, be encouraged that you have more options than you might think! In Chapter 5, we'll continue to use the blues as a tool for learning new facets of the music.

CHAPTER 5

LIVING IN HARMONY: THE ♭9TH AND ♭13TH

In Chapter 3, we discussed extended chords, or chord "tensions," where notes from the relative scale were added above the chord tones. To expand on that, let's begin to examine alterations to these tensions, starting with the ♭9th.

As you remember, a 9th tension is the same note as the second degree of the scale. A ♭9th is just that—a flatted, or lowered, second degree of the major scale.

The ♭9th is almost exclusively paired with a dominant chord (e.g., C7♭9).

	1	♭2	**3**	4	**5**	♭6	♭**7**	8 (1)	♭**9**
C7♭9	**C**	D♭	**E**	F	**G**	A♭	**B♭**	C	**D♭**

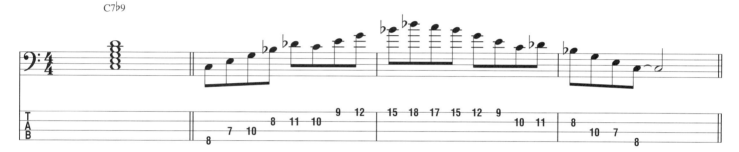

Another common chord tension you'll see on dominant chords in jazz is the ♭13th, which is the same note as the flatted sixth degree of the scale.

	1	♭2	**3**	4	**5**	♭6	♭**7**	8 (1)	♭9	3	11	5	♭**13**
C7♭13	**C**	D♭	**E**	F	**G**	A♭	**B♭**	C	D♭	E	F	G	**A♭**

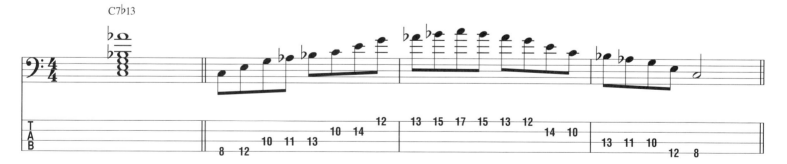

It's important to note that just because chord tension names like 9 and 13 extend above the octave does not mean that they must be played in a higher register. A bassist can use these notes in any range of the instrument, in both solos and walking bass lines.

Let's use these altered tensions in our next Technique Tune-Up.

TECHNIQUE TUNE-UP: STRING RAKING AND TRIPLET DROPS

To add movement and interest to a line or solo phrase, the technique of "raking" across the strings is a good option to have at our disposal. It's a simple concept, but very effective when used properly. It serves to fill space between very large intervals as you jump from high to low, is a helpful way to execute "triplet drops," and generally gives an extra sense of propulsion to the rhythmic feel.

The technique is created by striking strings from high to low in quick succession using only one finger of your plucking hand. So, rather than playing each string one at a time, your hand should be drawn in one motion across the strings. Use this first exercise to familiarize yourself with the concept and build comfort with the movement.

TRACK 41

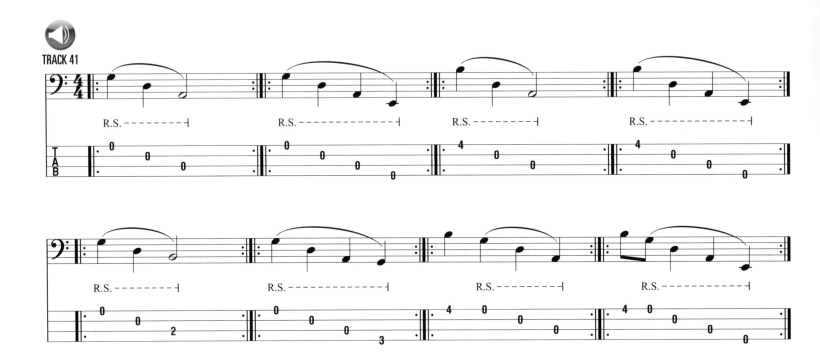

As mentioned, raking strings is useful when making a large interval jump from high to low. Here are some examples that you can play through to understand the idea, using the altered dominant chord that we learned in the previous section. Notice that, in bar 3 of the third example, we are playing an A♮ instead of the ♭9th, A♭, to maintain a smooth string rake.

TRACK 42

Moderately

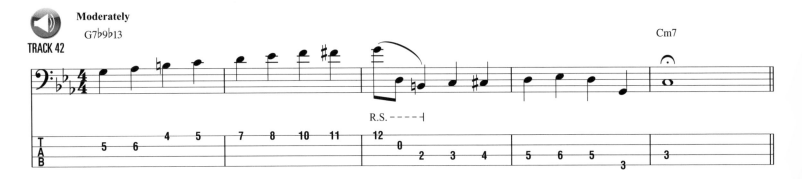

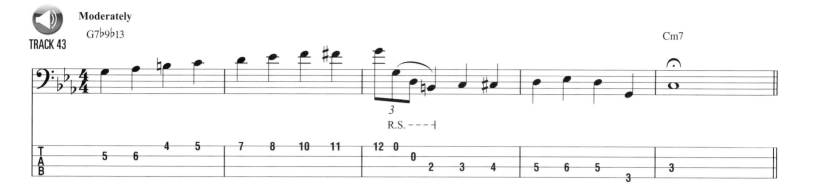

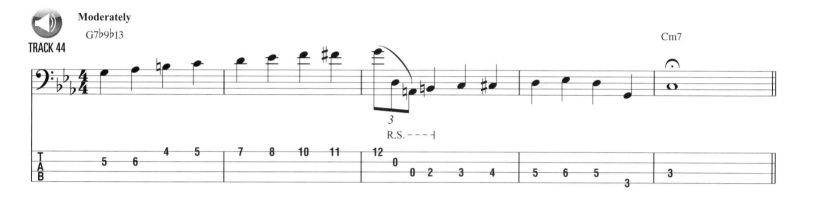

Raking strings is one way to perform a **triplet drop**, which we incorporated in some of the previous examples. Let's isolate a few examples in the following exercise:

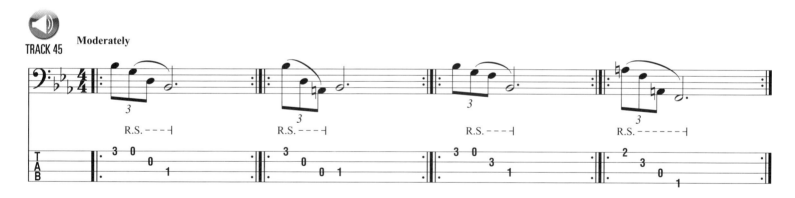

Below are examples of some phrases that you might play in a solo or a bass fill while accompanying another instrument. The use of the string rake here can help make playing these kinds of musical statements easier.

We'll see the triplet drop and string rake in the Bass Accompaniment section of this chapter, but before we get there, let's first learn about minor blues.

CHANGES ARE INEVITABLE: THE MINOR BLUES

Nearly identical in form to the major blues we explored in Chapter 4, the minor blues typically maintains the former's 12-bar structure but is comprised of minor chords instead of major or dominant ones. The harmonic progression also stays broadly the same.

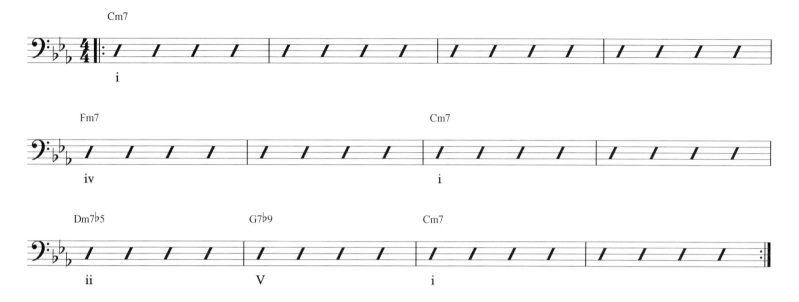

Notice that not only are the I and IV chords minor, but the ii–V looks different from what we've seen before. These alterations of the chord qualities and tensions are to maintain the relative sound of the key center. Since C minor is the relative minor key of E♭ major, we have the note A♭ to contend with. Building the D minor and G dominant seventh chords, we reference the relative key by incorporating the A♭ into the chord construction.

One common alternative to these exact chord changes involves a substitution of the iim7♭5 chord in measure 9. To present a slightly smoother movement to the V7, we utilize what's called a **tritone substitution**. This is an often-used replacement for chords with a dominant function. The tritone substitution, or "tritone sub," is created by building a dominant seventh chord on the root that is a tritone away from the original chord. In the example below, the A♭7 replaces the Dm7♭5. These tritone subs work because there are so many shared notes between the substitute and original chord.

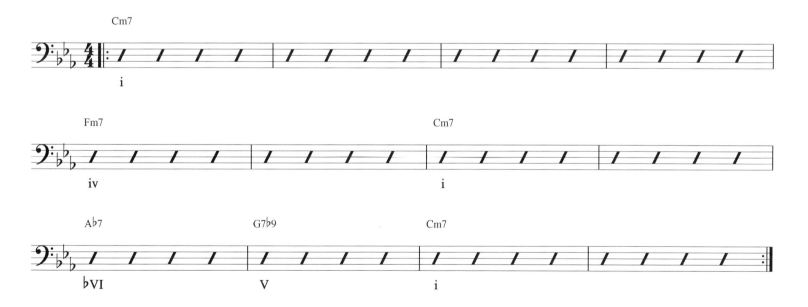

A final addition to our minor blues is the use of a **secondary dominant** in measure 4. This isn't unique to minor blues but is a good opportunity to touch on this concept. Secondary dominants add diversity to the harmony by creating temporary emphasis on one of the chords in the progression, regardless of the key of the moment. Below, you'll see a ii7♭5–V7♭9 (often called a "minor ii–V") in bar 4 that steps "outside" of the C minor key and creates a dominant pull to the Fm7 chord in bar 5.

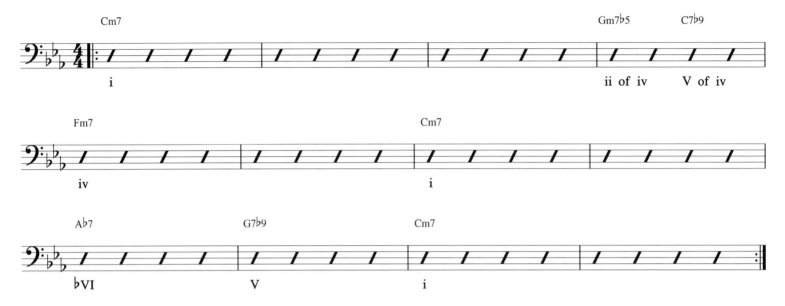

We'll use a minor blues in the next section to study a unique way of accompanying with the bass.

BASS ACCOMPANIMENT: THE OSTINATO

An **ostinato**—a repeated note, riff, or pattern within a song—is a technique that can add a feeling of suspense or hesitation while comping. This tension is then released by returning to a walking bass line. Let's examine some ways of incorporating ostinatos into bass lines with this example of a D minor blues.

A simple application of this idea involves playing a portion of a walking bass line repeatedly for effect. Notice the dynamic change when shifting back to conventional walking in the second chorus.

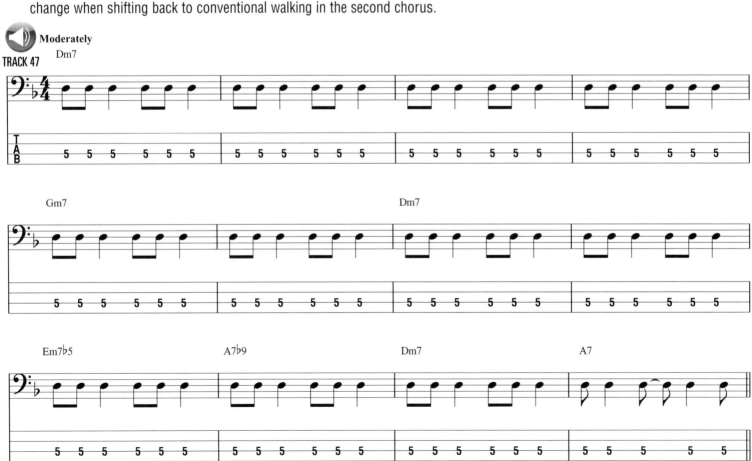

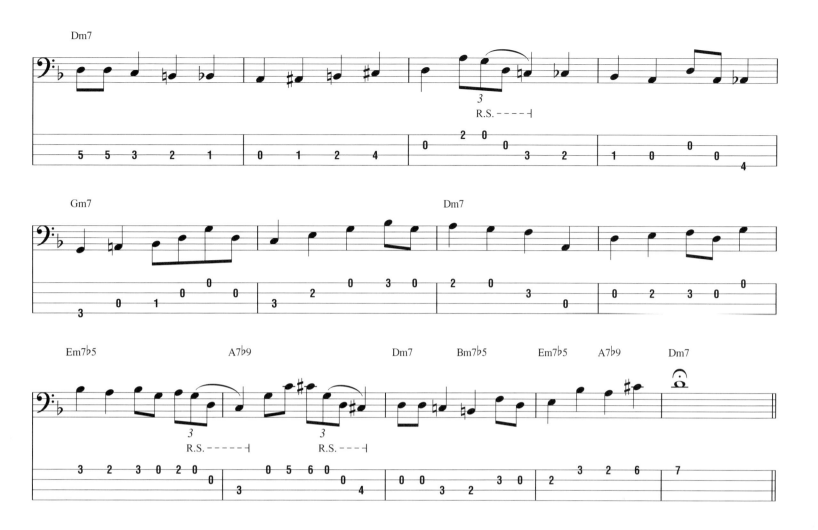

Another useful manifestation of this concept is to create a small, repetitive melody during the walking bass line that involves more than just quarter notes. When utilized appropriately, this can be an excellent way to participate in the musical conversation while maintaining the primary role as accompanist.

While an ostinato is technically defined as an exact repetition of a phrase, the term can be used more freely. For example, when riffs are transposed to fit different chord changes, the entire bass line can be referred to as an "ostinato." In the example below, notice that you can apply the raking technique to the descending part of the line.

You may also choose to insert an ostinato in your line to create dissonance and suspense. By playing a repetitive figure that clashes with the stated harmony, a sense of musical strain is created. Notice below that the various note choices are not the roots of the chords themselves, but rather other chord tones. To maintain the musical idea through the chorus, we include some passing notes to connect one non-root chord tone to another.

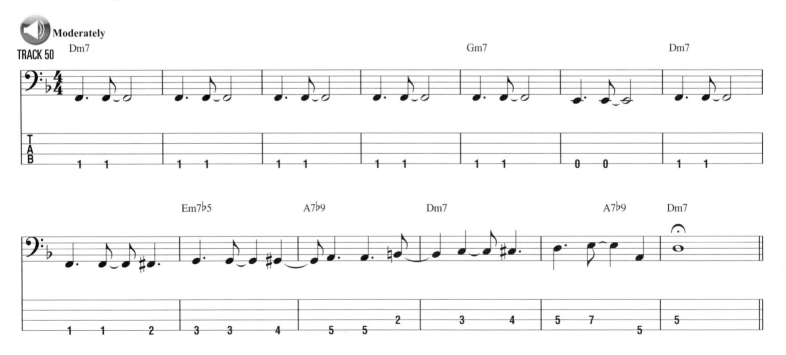

PREPARING TO SOLO: SCALES FOR THE ♭9TH AND ♭13TH

Earlier in this chapter, we learned about the altered tensions ♭9th and ♭13th. Let's look at some scales that we can use over chords with these tensions. Since these alterations occur almost always with dominant chords, and the Mixolydian mode is always a good foundation for that chord quality, let's begin there.

For a scale that works well with a dominant 7♭9 chord, simply lower the second degree of the Mixolydian scale by a half step:

Likewise, for a scale that will compliment a dominant 7♭13 chord, lower the sixth degree:

When both tensions are in the chord, we can use the Mixolydian ♭9 ♭13 scale shown below. This scale also happens to be the fifth mode of the F harmonic minor scale, or in other words, the same notes as the F harmonic minor scale, starting on C.

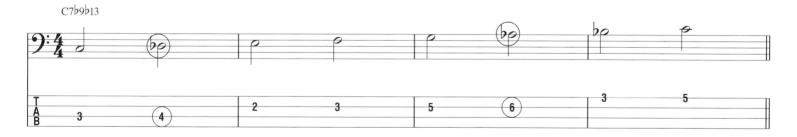

Now let's learn a new soloing concept, using these altered tensions in our melodies.

ALL EARS ON YOU: TELLING A STORY

A good story is something that grabs your attention early and allows you to follow along with every twist and turn. It has naturally occurring events that involve consequence, action and reaction, and contrast. It also has elements of surprise that allow the audience to expect one thing yet get another.

In musical terms, we would refer to this idea as "theme and development" or "motivic development."

A **motif** is a single musical idea in a generally small unit in time. Motifs are often followed by a brief period of rest in order to distinguish them as individual statements. By creating a motif and applying various adjustments to it, our solos take on understandable and interesting progressions that are enjoyable to listen to.

After playing the following motif which uses the ♭9th and ♭13th tensions we learned earlier, we'll vary the original phrase by amending the note choices but maintaining the rhythm:

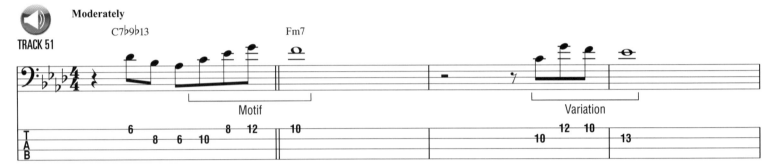

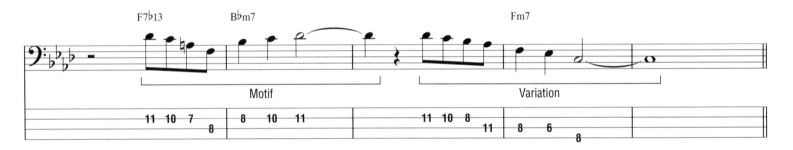

Another option is to extend the motif: Play the original phrase, rest, then play the phrase again but extend the melodic idea on the second time through.

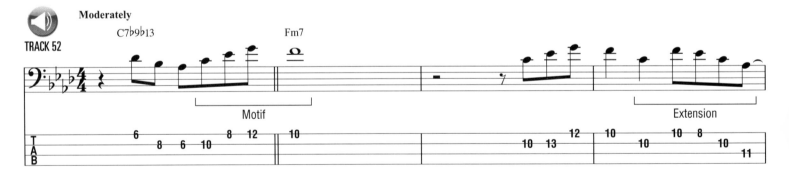

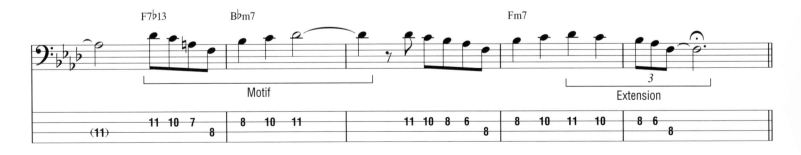

If we play a slightly longer or multi-motive phrase, we can build on the idea by resting and then repeating a section of the original phrase. So, we'll play a portion of the original idea instead of repeating the whole motif:

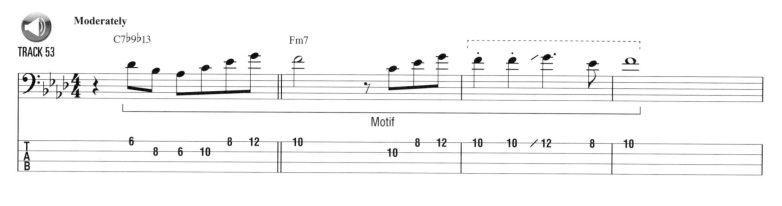

Combining these ideas, we can state an original theme, rest, repeat a portion of it, and then immediately add material to the fragmented section:

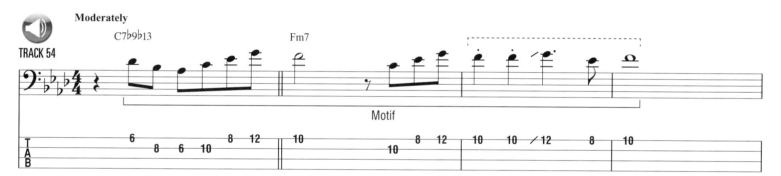

One more idea is to add elements of rhythmic variation to the restatement of the motif or fragment. Maintain the same notes or note shape, but condense or expand the rhythmic pattern:

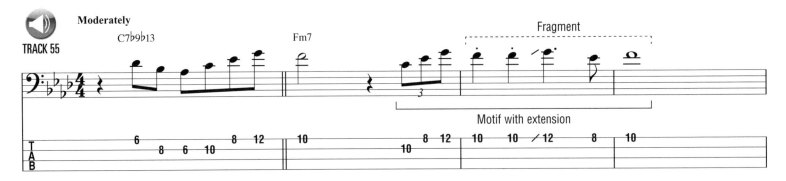

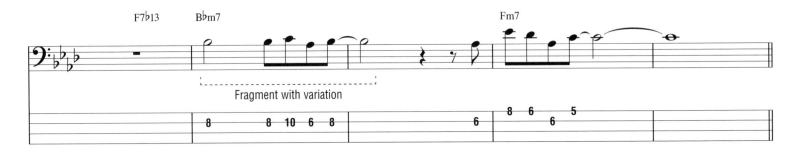

Now when someone asks you to "tell a story" in your soloing, you'll know where to start!

CHAPTER 6

LIVING IN HARMONY: THE #9TH AND #11TH

Chord changes in a jazz blues often have other manipulated extensions. Chapter 5 introduced us to altering tensions by lowering them one half step. Now let's look at the same principle, but this time we'll raise the extensions by a half step.

Like the ♭9th, the #9th is commonly seen as an altered extension of a dominant seventh chord. And, like the blues scales we discussed earlier, the "rub" of the #9th (enharmonically equivalent to [i.e., it's the same pitch as] the ♭3rd) against the natural 3rd of the dominant chord gives the harmony a mournful quality. Below is the chord's construction in its most basic form. Note that the notes/numbers in the chart represent what is essentially the Mixolydian mode with a raised 9th.

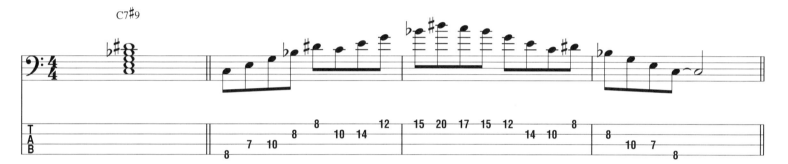

The #11th is the first tension we've examined that is very often used on other chord qualities, in addition to dominant sevenths. For example, maj7#11 chords are used in many compositions.

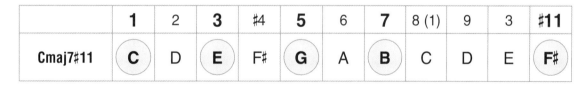

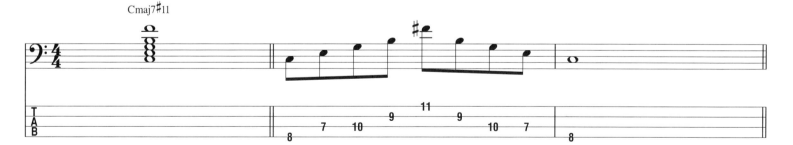

To create a dominant seventh chord with a #11 (C7#11), just flat the 7th of the arpeggio above.

Let's explore these altered tensions in this chapter's Technique Tune-Up, where we'll look at several ways to add vocal-like qualities to our sound.

TECHNIQUE TUNE-UP: EMULATING THE HUMAN VOICE

While improvisation isn't unique to jazz, one thing that does separate it from other music genres is the singular, personal quality that we seek in our performance.

Over time, and as we strive to master various skills, we develop individual preferences for the way that we phrase, the notes that we choose, and the rhythmic feeling that we embody. Ultimately, you will select different tools and combinations of techniques while searching for "your sound."

The human voice, with its enormous range of expression, is one such sound that we can certainly try to emulate to achieve that goal. When an instrument is played with a vocal quality, there is an organic reflection of the natural breath of life. As listeners, we are instinctively drawn towards the sound of a cooing baby or the wail of someone in pain. Can we find a way to imitate these sounds on our instrument?

On the bass, we have the ability to slide in and around notes, bend into or out of them, and attack them in a variety of ways.

A **scoop** is a vocal-like slide up to a desired pitch. You can begin a scoop at different distances from a target pitch, but make sure that the rhythm remains strong.

Another useful device is the **pull-off**, which is performed by plucking a fretted note and then "pulling off" the fret-hand finger to make a nearby note ring.

A **hammer-on** is the opposite of a pull-off. Still within one fingerboard position, the first note is plucked, and then the next, higher note is sounded by "hammering" onto it with a fret-hand finger.

We can also use **glissando** to good effect, especially if mimicking the human voice. A short "fall-off" gives the note extra flavor.

One very clever idea that a colleague suggested to me was to attempt to transcribe and imitate traditional blues vocalists. By trying to copy the exact phrasing and nuances of artists like Son House, Skip James, or Robert Johnson, we can become much more intimately involved with the qualities of the human voice.

The ♯9th and ♯11th alterations that we learned earlier make great fodder for these techniques. Because of the half-step movement from the ♯9th to the ♭3rd, and from the ♯11th to the ♭5th, we've got logical and comfortable note choices that make sense and sound great.

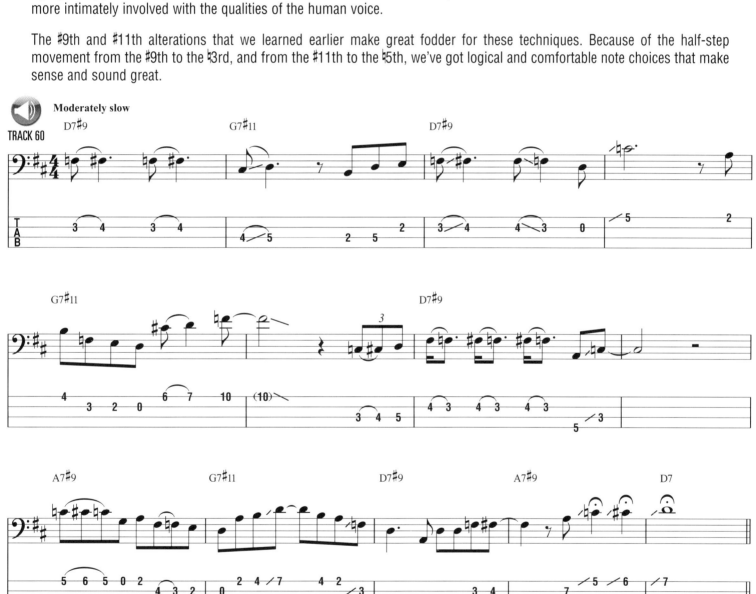

Certainly, don't limit yourself to the blues genre! For example, if you try to notate the phrasing of Louis Armstrong, you'll find that it is an exercise in futility. The breadth of subtlety in his performances defy conventional notation. However, you can still copy him with your ears and try to assimilate the freedom and creativity that he possessed.

The great Charlie Parker also embodied this kind of liberty and originality. Let's explore one way that he influenced the blues.

CHANGES ARE INEVITABLE: "BIRD" BLUES

Charlie "Yardbird" Parker, most often simply referred to as "Bird," was a saxophone player who redefined jazz. As one of the main creators of a jazz style called "bebop," Bird's influence changed the direction of the music forever. While there are limitless things to learn from Bird, in this section, we're going to examine a unique set of alterations to the blues that he created.

Just as musicians added more sophisticated chords to the earliest blues changes, Charlie Parker expanded the harmony even further in a composition called "Blues for Alice." And his changes were so logical, hip, and fun to play that they became a staple of the jazz repertoire. Musicians often apply these same chords to other blues tunes, and often-played songs like Bird's "Confirmation" and Toots Thielemans' famous "Bluesette" feature this harmonic progression.

"Blues for Alice" maintains the traditional 12-bar form, and the primary harmonic moments of a typical blues remain the same, as well. It's the connection between these moments that make the progression special. Take a look at the chord changes below, which are in the style of "Blues for Alice" and include a relatively simple walking bass line for reference.

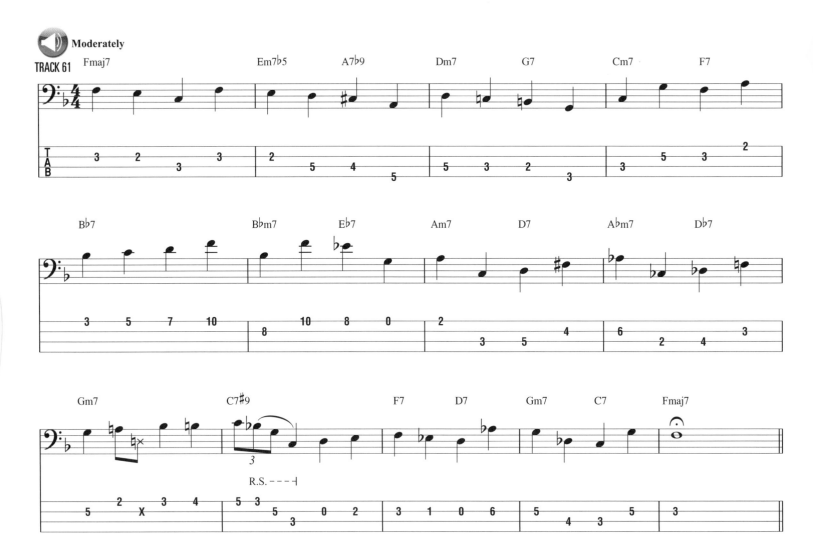

Remember that, earlier in our discussions of harmony, we talked about the importance of the ii–V–I progression and how additions to the strong V–I resolution sound can provide more sonic colors to explore. An analysis of the so-called "Bird Blues" changes reveals these points.

As alluded to above, the I chord, IV chord, and ii–V progressions of a typical blues all occur in their usual places, but Bird added a series of chords in between that provide interest and harmonic possibilities.

Notice that the chords in measures 2–4 all lead to bar 5 in a cycle of ii–Vs. Rather than resolving to the tonic, each V7 chord deceptively "resolves" to the iim7 chord of the next ii–V before finally landing on the IV chord (Bb7). In the next portion of harmonic movement, the ii–Vs in bars 6–8 move downward in half steps to arrive at Gm7, their point of resolution. On a smaller scale, each measure leads smoothly to the next, like the cogs of an analog watch that feed into one another.

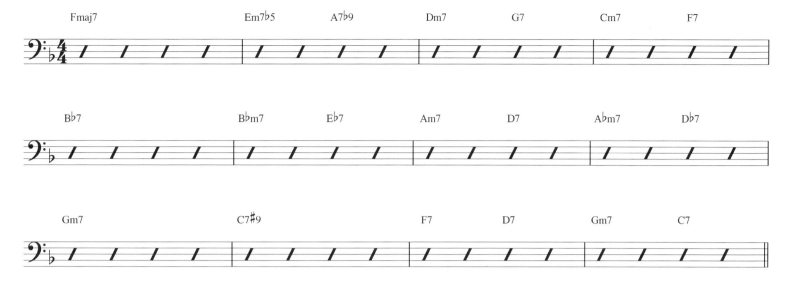

A few points of interest: the first chord is a major seventh rather than the typical dominant seventh of the blues; the melody to "Blues for Alice" actually contains a B natural in bar 2, though the chord (Em7♭5) is usually played as written; measure 10 isn't typically notated with the ♯9, but the melody of the song does contain a strong example of this altered tension.

Like the typical blues form itself, the "Bird blues" progression is important to study, practice, and play. It is not only an extremely common part of the shared jazz repertoire, but it provides us with new ways to expand our harmonic vocabulary.

BASS ACCOMPANIMENT: CHORD SUBSTITUTION

In jazz music, the walking bass line can be a powerful force in defining the harmony of a song. A bassist has the power to control a broad range of harmonic possibilities and can redirect the entire performance of a tune, all while playing just one note at a time.

The act of manipulating the harmony with our bass notes is something we usually do naturally, though it is often very understated. Every time we play the 5th of a chord, we are implying—albeit subtly—the dominant chord on that beat. Below are some examples that demonstrate how we might choose to "reharmonize" the chord changes in a very deliberate way.

The first substitution revolves around the ii–V–I cadence. Remember that, because the notes that make up the iim7 chord in a given key are shared by the V7, we can always imply the iim7 where a dominant chord exists. This will add a bit more color to the harmony and slightly delay the sound of the dominant chord. Substituted chords are shown in italics above the original harmony in the following examples.

Chromaticism, or movement in half steps, is a staple of walking bass lines. When we are thinking of the harmony that we may be adding to a tune, chromatic lines take on additional weight.

Diatonic substitutions are another way to add motion to the harmonic progression. Here, we're inserting chords derived from the keys of E♭ major in the first example below and A♭ major in the second.

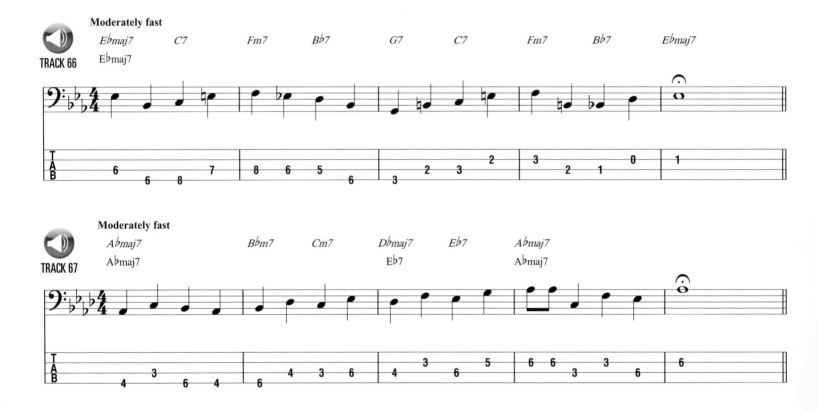

Tritone substitutions are also commonly alluded to in our bass lines. Because the tritone sub contains the same tritone interval of the dominant seventh chord that it is replacing, and the root of the substitution usually creates chromatic movement in the bass line, it's an extremely strong and effective sound to use.

Here are two examples that implement tritone substitutions:

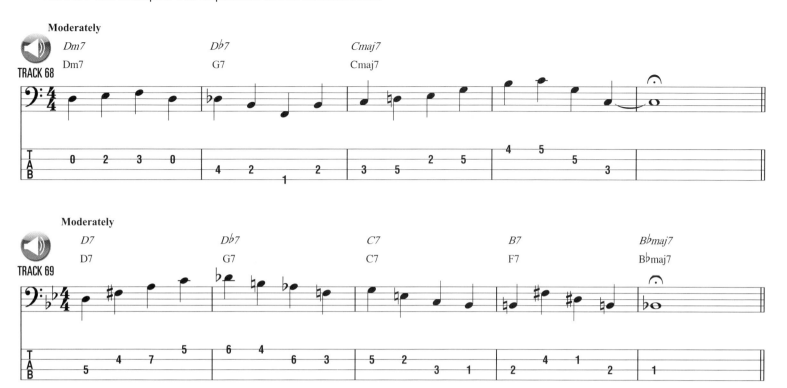

When we examine what different bass notes can do to change the harmony that exists on top of the root, there is a nearly limitless variety of options available. Master bassist Ron Carter has developed this skill so profoundly that his reharmonizations can be songs in and of themselves.

In that same way, Charlie Parker created "Blues for Alice" as an entirely new way of playing the blues. Let's use our new concepts to look at a few substitutions that we can place over "Bird blues" changes.

By understanding harmonic function, movement, and theory, we can bring dynamic additions to our performances via our bass line note choices.

PREPARING TO SOLO: SCALES FOR THE ♯9TH AND ♯11TH

As you've no doubt already discovered, there are a great deal of variations available with respect to harmony and theory. While I would prefer to include every single variable in this method book, the responsibility will have to fall on you to continue gathering information from as many sources as you can. That said, here are a few scales that you can use when you encounter ♯9th and ♯11th chords in your soloing.

Our initial choice for a dominant 7♯9 chord might be the basic Mixolydian mode with a raised 9th (or 2nd), as represented in the chart earlier in the chapter.

Another option available to solo on a 7♯9 chord is the **altered scale**, also called the "super-Locrian" or "diminished whole-tone" scale. This scale contains the ♭9th, ♯9th, ♯11th, and ♯5th.

C Altered Scale

The ♮5th (G♮) of the C7 chord isn't represented in the altered scale. That's alright if your intention is clear and you don't want to include or emphasize the G♮. If you do want to highlight it, though, you might also consider the following series of notes, the **symmetrical diminished scale**, also called the "half-whole diminished" scale. In this scale, the half-step/whole-step pattern repeats continuously, giving us the natural fifth along with both altered 9ths and the ♯11th. Also, notice that it contains eight notes before the octave rather than the usual seven.

C Diminished Scale

We'll explore diminished scales at length in the next chapter.

To review, our scale choices for a 7♯9 chord are Mixolydian ♯9, altered, and symmetrical diminished (half-whole). Now let's examine some scales appropriate for chords with the ♯11th tension.

In our earlier discussion of the ♯11th, recall that we used a maj7♯11 chord and found that we can easily place the standard Lydian mode over this chord. There are, of course, many other places where you'll encounter the ♯11th, with a dominant seventh chord being one of the most common.

For the ♯9th, you can easily use the three scales that we just reviewed, as they all contain the ♯11th, as well. But perhaps you'd rather not imply such dense chromaticism. In these cases, the **Lydian dominant scale** works perfectly.

C Lydian Dominant Scale

Derived from the fourth degree of the melodic minor scale (in this example, G melodic minor), I find this scale more easily understood as a basic Mixolydian scale with a ♯11th. When a dominant chord contains only this alteration, Lydian dominant should be a useful go-to scale.

ALL EARS ON YOU:
THE RIGHT NOTES IN THE RIGHT PLACES

Consider what makes a melody: a sequence of single notes, generally laid out in a musical way, and most often with a defined rhythm of some kind. For somewhat mysterious reasons, we are drawn to creating and hearing melodies that we define as pleasing, compelling, or fulfilling. There are as many ways of defining these terms as there are individual listeners, and so you're ultimately the arbiter of good taste with respect to your own improvised melodies.

We should, however, develop the knowledge and skill to manipulate melodies in any way that we find artistically important, and to do so, we need to delve deeply into mastering melodic content.

When we improvise, we should ultimately be able to "hear" the notes or melodies in our head before playing them. To do so, we need to become intimately familiar with the colors of different notes in relation to harmony and each other. You can practice this concept by playing a chord, say on piano, and then singing or playing notes and all their different alterations on top, one at a time. With repetition, this exercise will train your ear to hear all the colors available to you for soloing.

Additionally, compose your own pieces when you can and attempt to use these new sounds in your composed melodies. You'll find that fighting for the perfect melody note over a specific chord change will force you to examine them all more closely.

Try the following exercise with various chord changes: focus entirely on one scale degree for a whole chorus, whether it's part of the chord spelling or not. For example, if you're trying to get a handle on the sound of a #11th, use that scale degree as much as possible within an improvised chorus.

The #11ths in this example are highlighted.

Keep in mind that the melody is king! We should be consistently striving for good melodies, regardless of a phrase's analytical meaning.

Here's one more solo over Bird blues changes, this time utilizing many of the concepts covered in this chapter, like #9th and #11th chords and their scales, chord substitutions, and vocal-style articulations.

Use the play-a-long version of the audio to create your own solos that focus on particular tensions and to practice the scales we learned. Having a very specific goal with respect to creating your solos will help in many ways!

CHAPTER 7

LIVING IN HARMONY: DIMINISHED AND HALF-DIMINISHED CHORDS

So far, we've seen some diminished chords in our examples and briefly touched on the symmetrical diminished scale. Additionally, half-diminished (m7b5) chords have appeared in some of our chord changes. In this section, and in this chapter as a whole, we'll look more in depth at each.

The unique diminished chord and its accompanying scales are a versatile and useful sound in many contexts. Created with a sequence of minor-3rd intervals, there's an inherent tension in the sound.

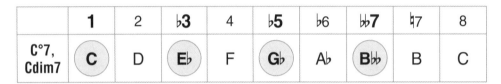

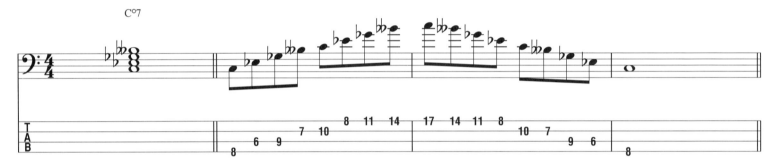

An important thing to note: the bb7th ("double-flat seventh") is technically correct in notation and analysis, but will most often be written as it's enharmonic equivalent for practical purposes. In the example above, the enharmonic equivalent of Bbb is A♮. This is a common "edit" of the technical spelling so that reading the notation is easier. From here forward, I'll use the enharmonic spelling in our examples.

The diminished concept involves a lot of interesting things, and we'll explore these throughout this chapter. Let's look now at the m7b5, or half-diminished, chord.

At its most basic level, the m7b5 is directly created from the Locrian mode of the major scale.

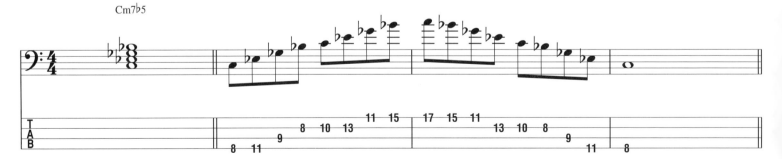

Notice that the construction is similar to the fully diminished chord, but rather than a ♭♭7th, the half-diminished chord features a ♭7th. The chord is essentially a minor seventh chord but with a ♭5th.

As always, practice these chords over every root, play them in all of their inversions, and integrate the sound into your inner ear as best you can.

TECHNIQUE TUNE-UP: PLAYING WITH THE BOW

Playing with the bow provides great benefits for our overall bass skills. Intonation, hand independence, and sound production are all bolstered with arco playing. Additionally, we have more sonic possibilities for our musical expression.

While the electric bass doesn't have the luxury of this playing option, all bassists would benefit from studying classical music masters like Domenico Dragonetti, Giovanni Bottesini, Serge Koussevitzky, Edgar Meyer, Francois Rabbath, and Gary Karr.

In jazz music, we have bassists like Jimmie Blanton, Leroy "Slam" Stewart, Paul Chambers, Israel "Cachao" Lopez, Ray Brown, and Christian McBride to emulate. These virtuosos utilize the bow to great effect while playing melodies, soloing, and adding color to a song.

While the rhythmic aspect of jazz differs from traditional classical music, the technique remains constant. One fundamental technique that we can focus on to honor that rhythmic difference is the choice of the bow stroke.

The **down-bow stroke** (⊓) involves drawing the bow towards your body, while an **up-bow stroke** (∨) sends the bow in the opposite direction.

Let's review the symmetrical whole-half diminished scale and mark the strokes in a "stable" way, playing two notes per stroke.

Now let's change the placement of the strokes. Notice how the line has more of a lilt, or feeling of forward motion.

Because you are accenting the upbeats, the feeling of the rhythm has a more dynamic pull. You can also begin the phrase on an upbeat:

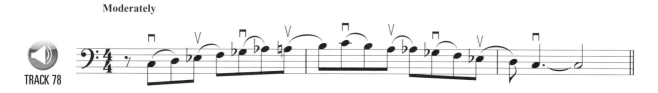

Now utilize an up-bow on the upbeat, and you should notice a natural inclination toward the swing feeling.

To further illustrate this point, let's use some more melodic phrases with the diminished and half-diminished chord scales that we learned. We'll begin with an up-bow and change the order of the strokes to really sit in the swing feeling.

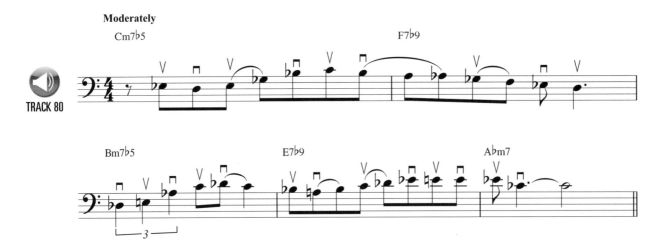

While some current bassists, like Christian McBride, still play arco as a regular part of their performance repertoire, it's not nearly as common in jazz settings as it used to be. However, there is one place where playing with the bow remains standard: in a ballad.

We'll look at ballads later in this chapter, but first let's explore common uses of the diminished chords that we learned in the previous section.

CHANGES ARE INEVITABLE: DIMINISHED CHORD APPLICATIONS

Now that we've been introduced to diminished chords, let's take a look at some common ways that they can be used in chord progressions. The first thing to note is that diminished chords often have a dominant function. Much like the dominant seventh chords we learned earlier, diminished chords have an "unstable" sound that wants to resolve.

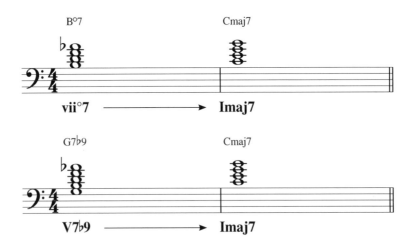

You'll notice in the example above that the diminished chord is essentially the same as the V7♭9 chord that we learned earlier. Here are a couple more examples:

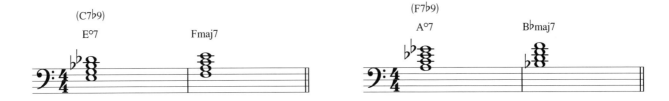

The diminished seventh chord can also resolve to a minor seventh chord:

When we think of diminished chords in this way, we are focusing on their harmonic function. Diminished chords can, however, serve as harmonic embellishment, without any specific function. This is commonly used when the we want a sense of movement during the duration of a static chord. While the resultant movement has tension and release, we don't consider these as part of the overall analysis of a harmonic progression.

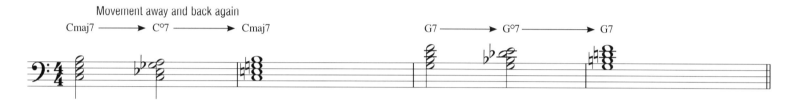

Examine the context of a diminished chord that you might encounter. If it resolves precisely as expected, you can consider it a functional diminished chord. If it does not, it is most likely an embellishment. There are instances, however, where diminished chords are both functional and act as embellishments: as part of an ascending or descending progression. The diminished chords below pull our ear in the direction of the progression and also connect two chords in a functional way.

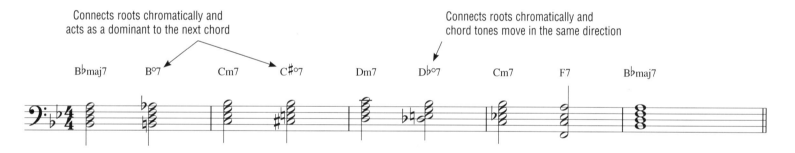

Let's use a similar progression in our Bass Accompaniment section pertaining to ballads…

BASS ACCOMPANIMENT: BALLAD BASICS

Many of us really miss taking advantage of the unique benefits of ballads. We've got the chance to investigate timbre, time feels, and melodic possibilities that we may miss in an up-tempo burner. A well-played ballad forces us to confront who we are as musicians and what we ultimately want to express.

The generic bass accompaniment in a ballad mimics much of the same ideas as a two-feel. We are generally playing roots on downbeats, mostly half notes, and doing our best to both support and push the ensemble forward. And, like the two-feel, we can use a variety of rhythmic choices to maintain interest and momentum in our accompaniment. Remember that one integral part of the history of jazz ballads is that they served as dance music, just as fast numbers did.

To further explore ballad-playing, let's examine two versions of the same chord progression. The first is slightly more grounded, while the second takes a few more "risks," providing some rhythmic twists and turns. This progression is similar to the first section of "Stella by Starlight," a popular jazz standard.

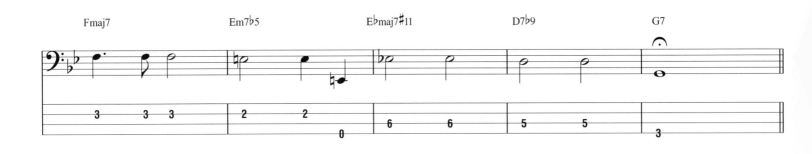

Remember earlier in this chapter, we learned that ballads are one place where arco playing is still common. Below is a typical example of using the bow in a ballad. The very last note, usually the root of the diatonic I chord, is held as a **fermata** with the ensemble. The bow allows us to extend the length of the held note as the tune comes to a close.

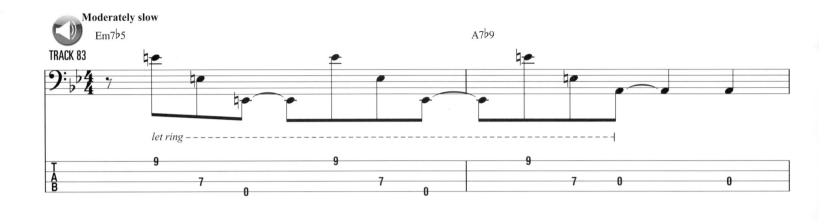

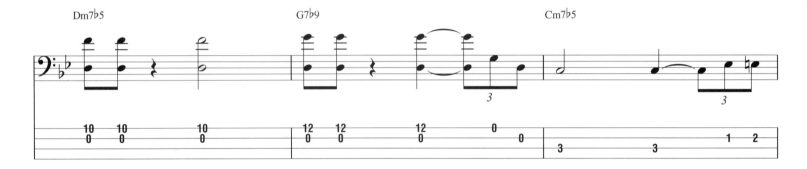

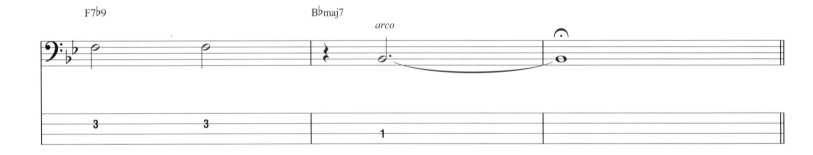

A satisfying way to explore arco playing is to play melodies in a ballad. This next bass line features examples of the diminished chord progression we studied earlier, including both ascending and descending harmonic movement.

Now let's take a closer look at some appropriate scales for the diminished and half-diminished chords so we can improvise our own melodies in a solo.

PREPARING TO SOLO:
SCALES FOR DIMINISHED AND HALF-DIMINISHED CHORDS

Investigating diminished scales is a perfect opportunity to emphasize the importance of the context of a chord in determining what notes to play. Let's examine each kind of scale, one at a time.

The **whole-half diminished scale** contains eight notes and is built with a consecutive series of alternating whole and half steps. This sequence of intervals gives the scale a unique symmetrical pattern and a sound that fits well with the diminished chord.

C Whole-Half Diminished Scale

The use of the whole-half diminished scale is usually dependent on its harmonic context. Generally, it's common to use this scale when:

- The diminished chord functions as a harmonic embellishment

- The root movement approaches a diatonic chord from above

- The melody of the song (or the composer) specifically dictates it

- The diminished chord lasts for a long time

- You are superimposing the scale over a dominant seventh chord that includes a ♭9th, ♯9th, or ♯11th

In another symmetrical arrangement of notes, the **half-whole diminished scale** is built beginning with a half step, and alternates between half and whole steps intervals up from the root note.

C Half-Whole Diminished Scale

The half-whole diminished scale is widely used with dominant seventh chords that include some or all the alterations: ♭9th, ♯9th, or ♯11th. It's rare to use this scale on other chord qualities, but you should experiment and see what you like!

Another diminished-type scale, the **diminished mode** is constructed from the seventh degree of the harmonic minor scale, but it's *not* symmetrical.

C Diminished Mode

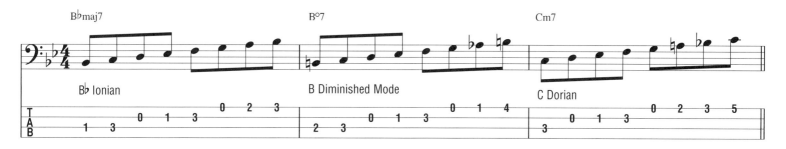

The diminished mode is an excellent choice when the harmony approaches a minor chord. It's especially useful in an ascending chromatic progression, like the one we looked at earlier.

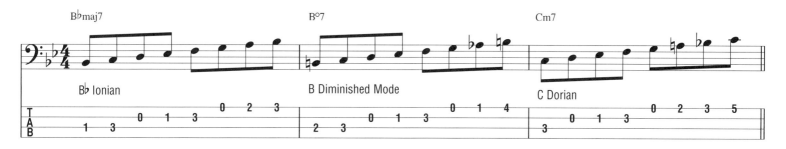

Remember, too, from our earlier discussion that a B°7 chord can also be considered a G7♭9 in terms of function. The notes have a strong pull to resolve, and, in this instance, specifically to a minor chord.

Our last part of this discussion is about the half-diminished, or m7♭5, chord. Generally speaking, we'll use either the Locrian mode or Locrian ♮9 (also called Locrian ♯2) scale, which is derived from the melodic minor scale.

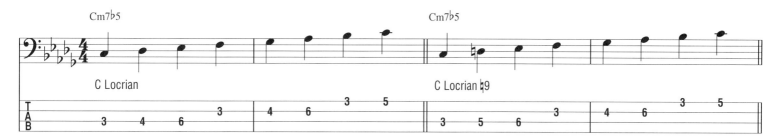

Be sure to practice these scales and familiarize yourself with their sounds in each key.

ALL EARS ON YOU: MAKING THE CHANGES

When improvising melodies, unless our intention is to overlay new harmony onto the existing song, we should strive to create lines that accurately reflect the sound of the written chords.

We call this "making" or "nailing" the changes, and this is especially clear when we select notes in the chord of the moment that were just previously not available. By "available," we mean the notes are either an alteration in the new, non-diatonic chord, or they are consonant on the current chord but would have been dissonant on the chord right before it.

Choosing the diminished and half-diminished scales based on the context we just discussed, and using the basic chord progression from earlier in the chapter, here is how those scales might be written out in the form. The arrows indicate important notes that are distinctive to the chord(s) in that bar, especially in the context of the chord that precedes it.

Because the tempo of ballads tends to allow for more space, this is a great vehicle for exploring the idea of making the changes by emphasizing unique, previously unavailable notes where we can. Take some time to analyze the specific choices in this exercise that reflect that. The C#/Db in bar 2, for example, is the first demonstration of this. Part of the E°7 chord spelling, this note would be very dissonant over the Ebmaj7 that begins the chorus (bar 1).

Notice that this solo doesn't follow a regimented formula, like playing a "special" note on the first beat of a bar or phrase, for example, but aims to express pleasing melodies while still using the unique notes of the moment. Try this exercise with many tunes and tempos, and for extra credit, play the melody in the example above with the bow!

CHAPTER 8

LIVING IN HARMONY: THE ♯5TH AND ♭5TH

Previously, we've discovered alterations mainly associated with other parts of the chord, but now let's focus our attention on constructing chords that manipulate the 5th specifically.

The ♯5th is found exclusively in major or dominant seventh chords. The maj7♯5 comes to us from the third mode of both the melodic minor and harmonic minor scales. Interestingly, it also appears in the rarely-referenced harmonic major scale. (Research this for extra credit!)

From the A harmonic minor scale:

	1	2	3	4	♯5	6	7	8
Cmaj7♯5 CM7♯5 C△7♯5	C	D	E	F	G♯	A	B	C

From the A melodic minor scale:

	1	2	3	♯4	♯5	6	7	8
Cmaj7♯5 CM7♯5 C△7♯5	C	D	E	F♯	G♯	A	B	C

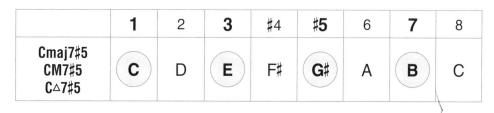

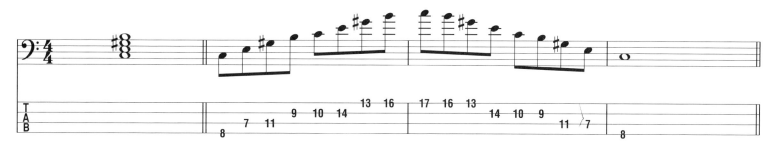

Dominant 7♯5 chords are associated with the six-note, symmetrical whole-tone scale. They resolve almost exclusively to a major chord, as the sharp 5th "pulls" toward the major 3rd.

	1	2	3	♯4	♯5	♯6/♭7	8
C7♯5	C	D	E	F♯	G♯	A♯/B♭	C

C7#5

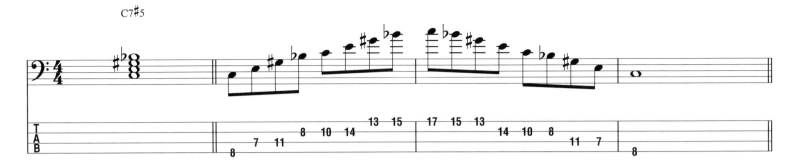

Additionally, we may consider that the dominant 7#5 is taken from the altered scale that we learned about in Chapter 6. This scale is also important when examining chords that have a ♭5th.

We've already encountered the ♭5th in diminished and half-diminished chords, but it can also be part of a dominant chord. Remember: this *replaces* the ♭5th. In this instance, the ♭5th does not function as a #11th, although the notes are enharmonically equivalent. As mentioned, we can consider the altered scale as this chord's "parent."

	1	♭2	#2	**3**	#4/♭**5**	#5/♭6	♭**7**	8
C7♭5	(C)	D♭	D#	(E)	F#/ (G♭)	G#/A♭	(B♭)	C

C7♭5

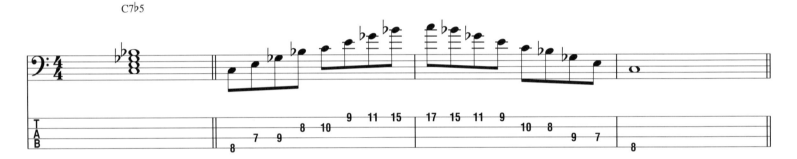

Lastly, you may sometimes see chord symbols written as a maj7♭5. While this chord is clearly used in compositions, its origin, parent scale, function, and chord scales are rather hotly contested. For the sake of simple demonstration, let's use the major scale but flat the 5th.

	1	2	**3**	4	♭**5**	6	**7**	8
Cmaj7♭5 **CM7♭5** **C△7♭5**	(C)	D	(E)	F	(G♭)	A	(B)	C

Cmaj7♭5

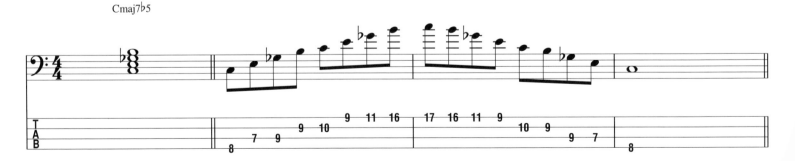

We will incorporate these harmonic considerations into our next Technique Tune-Up.

TECHNIQUE TUNE-UP: THUMB POSITION

So far, our focus has centered on notes in the middle-to-lower register of the bass. We would, however, be omitting a wide range of sonic possibilities without addressing notes in the higher range of the instrument. As mentioned previously, this register is usually easier for the average listener to hear and makes for a strong choice when soloing in particular.

While the above is true for both electric and upright basses, it's the upright that requires a more dramatic change in technique to play these notes. For this reason, the following section will be more relevant for upright bass players, however, electric bassists can follow along with the music examples for arpeggio practice.

Thumb position notes are conventionally thought of as those that reside above the open strings' upper octave point, for instance, above the high G on the G string. This playing position is named as such because the thumb is used in conjunction with other fingers to push down strings on the fingerboard.

In thumb position on the upright, the thumb, first, second, and third fingers are used to play notes. The fourth finger gets a break from its typically busy workload! By bringing our whole fretting arm around the neck of the bass and slightly leaning the bass back into our body, we're able to easily access this higher range of pitches. Proper hand placement will naturally lead us to use the side of the thumb to fret a note.

Be aware that as you climb higher on the range of the instrument, the individual notes become closer together on the fingerboard.

Take some time to slowly examine the ergonomics of shifting into and out of thumb position on the upright. Go *very* slowly and study how you must prepare your hand and arm, continue through the movement, and end up in proper position. Play these examples completely out of time and follow a qualified instructor's guidance to refine this technique.

Take note of the left-hand fingerings above each notehead. Tab is provided here for electric bass to play the arpeggios, but does not reflect the positions and fingerings given for the upright.

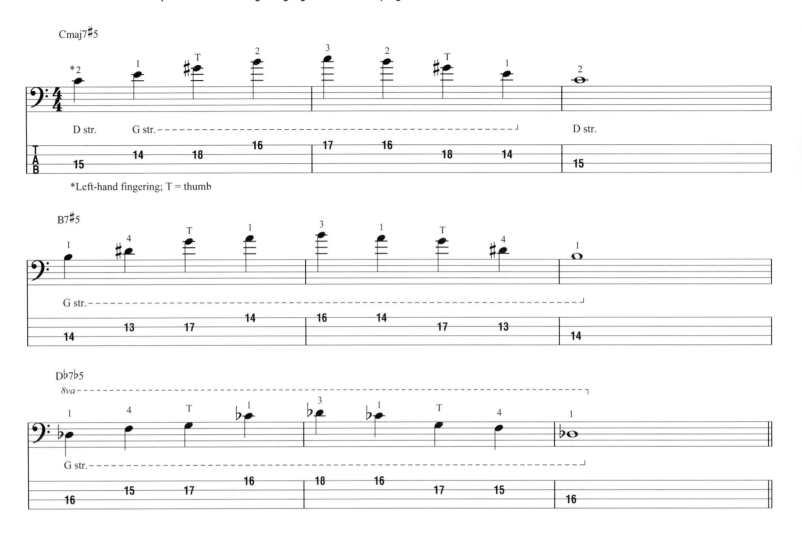

Here's an example that shows how to navigate the same arpeggios we just played while staying in thumb position and utilizing adjacent strings.

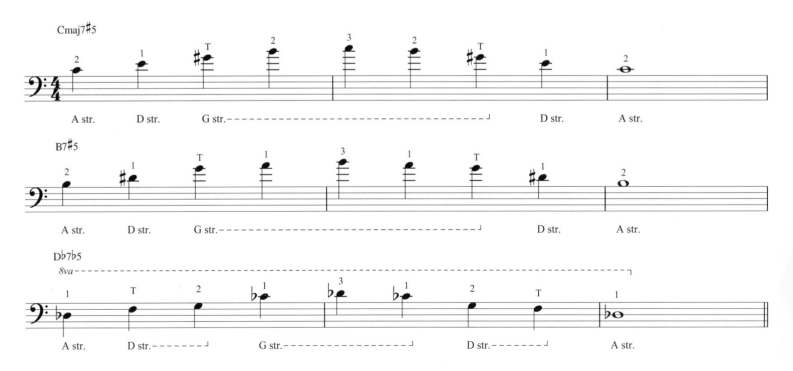

Using the chords from the previous examples plus the maj7♭5, let's connect the ideas of shifting into thumb position and then using adjacent strings by playing the following arpeggios in two octaves:

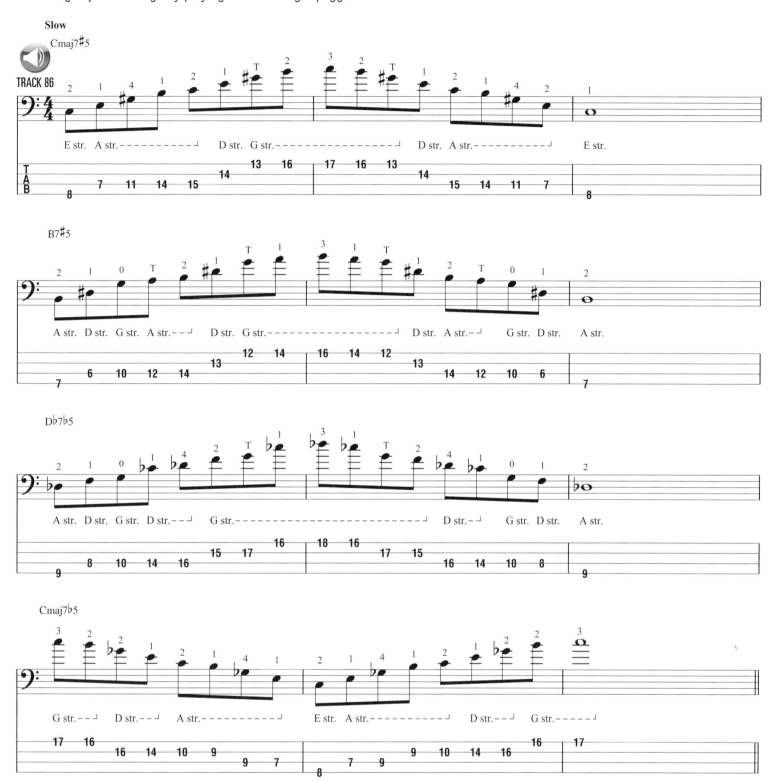

Let's give our thumbs a little break now as we examine a new chord progression in our next section…

CHANGES ARE INEVITABLE:
THE CYCLE-OF-4THS PROGRESSION

You've no doubt already studied, performed, or heard chord progressions based on the cycle of 4ths. Used in a large variety of ways in many, many compositions, this pleasing harmonic movement is both logically strong and open enough to be interpreted in countless ways.

The fundamental concept is the aural "pull" from one chord, especially if it's dominant, to a chord with a root that is an interval of a 4th above. An E7, for example, strongly wants to move to a chord with an A as its root (and often major, as we learned earlier). However, because we value surprise and variety in music, the chord quality can often be a *deceptive resolution.* That same E7 can just as commonly resolve to an A7 instead of an Amaj7.

Following our logic, that A7 naturally wants to move to its relative tonic, D. But if that D is a D7, the cycle continues, pulling towards G, and so on.

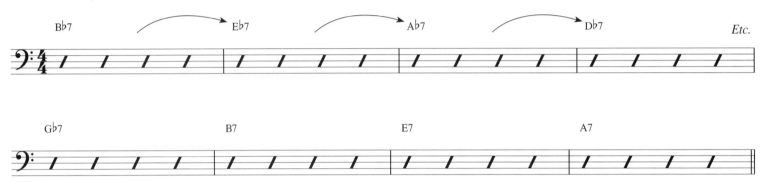

This type of chord progression can be found in many rhythmic variations and in various parts of a song's structure as you'll soon see.

Furthermore, the overall idea remains constant despite the actual chord qualities themselves. It's the *root movement* that we recognize as the cycle of 4ths.

We'll often see more colorful additions to the cycle. When analyzing a tune, remind yourself to look at broader sections to understand the internal structure. The following example is a ii–V–I progression moving through a cycle of 4ths.

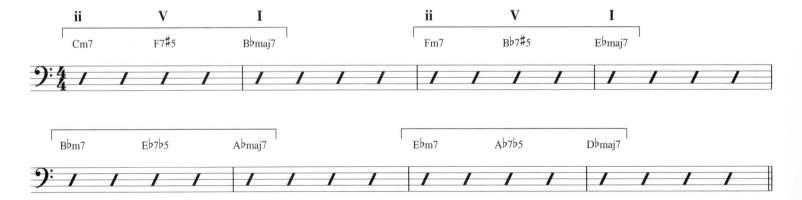

In Chapter 5, we briefly touched on tritone substitution as a tool for harmonic variety. If we apply this to our cycle of 4ths, we can create some clever chromatic bass movement:

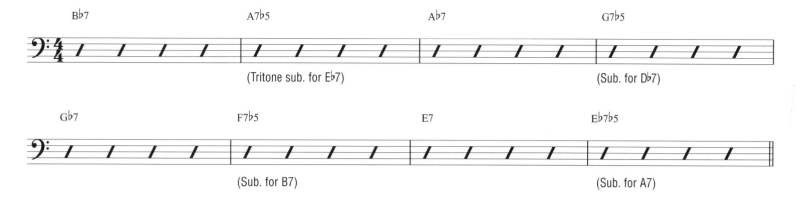

This is just a preliminary introduction to the ways in which the cycle of 4ths can be used. Be on the lookout in your studies for this harmonic relationship. It occurs so frequently, but in so many variations, you might not recognize it at first!

We'll stick with this concept as we look at bass accompaniment in 3/4 time.

BASS ACCOMPANIMENT: THE JAZZ WALTZ

So far, we've been using common time in our study examples, but of course, songs come in a variety of meters.

Playing in 3/4 time as a jazz waltz requires more than simply eliminating a quarter note from 4/4. The jazz-waltz feel has a distinct rhythmic quality that should maintain the buoyancy of swing while alluding to the common sensation of perceiving the time in "1." The underlying triplet motion should remain constant throughout, even though half notes and dotted quarter notes are often played.

Work through this first example with a sparse bass line to get acquainted with the idea of playing broadly through the chord changes, feeling a strong "1" at the beginning of each bar. Longer notes can be especially effective when playing a fast song in 3/4 time. Also, notice the cycle of 4ths progression in the first four measures.

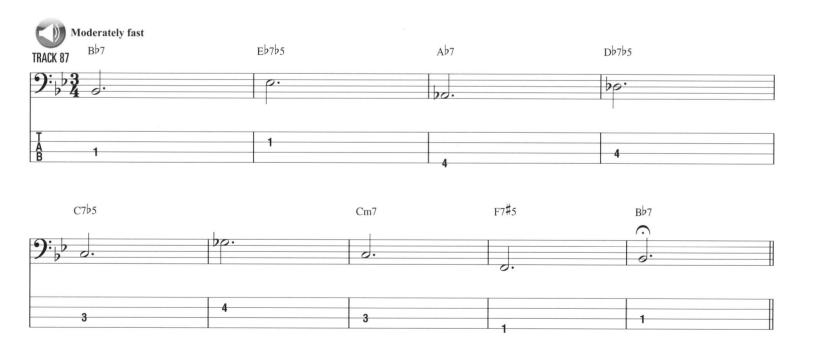

Similar to ornamenting a two-feel, you can add quarter notes and eighth notes to your lines to help to define the time and keep the line moving in a musical way.

Moderately fast

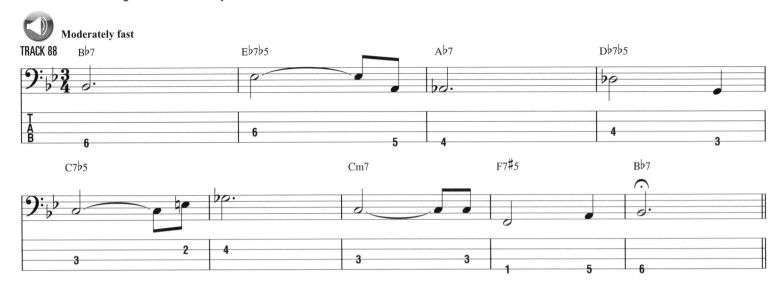

Playing a dotted-quarter-note feel in a jazz waltz is one more way to rhythmically embellish the bass line. Two dotted quarter notes split a bar of 3/4 evenly, which allows us to hint at multiple meters (two beats over three).

Moderately fast

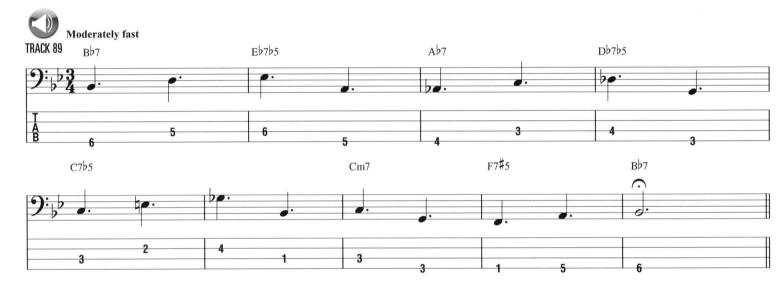

Of course, we can also play quarter notes:

Moderately fast

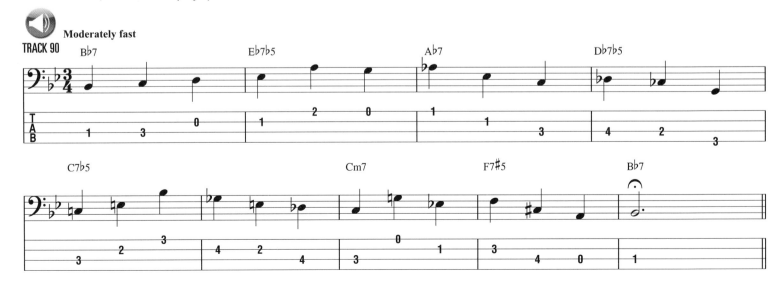

Here is an example of an active waltz bass line that combines these the devices:

We should always be thinking about how we arrange our own accompaniment while playing a song. It's important for everyone on the bandstand to take responsibility not only for the time and playing well with each other, but also for working to shape each song with dynamics, tension and release, and interest for the listener. I've found it effective to use the types of subdivisions listed above to slowly build tension that can be released later with walking quarter notes when the timing is right.

PREPARING TO SOLO: THE ALTERED AND WHOLE-TONE SCALES

There are two commonly used scales that contain both the ♭5th and the ♯5th from our chords in this chapter: the **whole-tone scale** and the **altered scale**.

We referenced the altered scale, sometimes called Super Locrian or the diminished whole-tone scale, in Chapter 6. It contains a ♭9th, ♯9th, 3rd, ♯11th/♭5th, ♯5th/♭13th, and ♭7th.

C Altered Scale

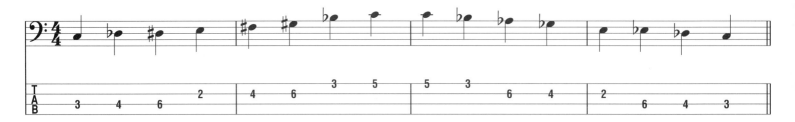

This scale can be superimposed over dominant chords that spell out the amended 5th, like a dominant 7♭5, or a chord marked "alt," like C7alt. This chord spelling with the "alt" suffix indicates that all the tensions from the altered scale are available to play.

The whole-tone scale, on the other hand, is a symmetrical scale like the diminished but is built with a sequence of consecutive major 2nd intervals.

C Whole-Tone Scale

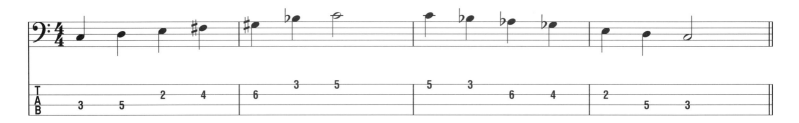

Whole-tone scales are almost always used with a dominant 7♯5 chord.

TWO WHOLE-TONE SCALES

Because of its construction of six equally-spaced notes, only two distinct sets of whole-tone scales can possibly be constructed within a 12-note music system: one with the notes C–D–E–F♯/G♭–G♯/A♭–A♯/B♭, and another a half step between with C♯/D♭–D♯/E♭–F–G–A–B.

There's an important distinction to be made when considering these chords and scales: technically speaking, a ♯11th is *not* the same as a ♭5th. While the notes may be harmonically identical, a chord spelling with a ♯11th indicates that there is a natural 5th in the chord. You may encounter instances in which a lead sheet or a discussion of harmony may indicate one or the other but may be inaccurately notated.

Pay close attention when encountering the ♭5th. Confirm the harmony by checking the melody, asking the composer, or conferring with others.

Next up, we'll combine these scales, chords, and waltz feel in an investigation into how we "phrase" melodies in our solos.

ALL EARS ON YOU: IMPROVISING WITH ALTERATIONS

We've come quite far in our list of chord tensions, alterations, and corresponding chord scales, so let's take a look now at how best to use these altered notes in our improvised melodies.

The following five examples are snippets from a full solo that appears on pages 108 and 109.

Our first step in beginning to apply alterations to a solo is to focus on the melody rather than the scale and choosing just one alteration to work with at a time. For our purposes, let's begin with the ♭9th.

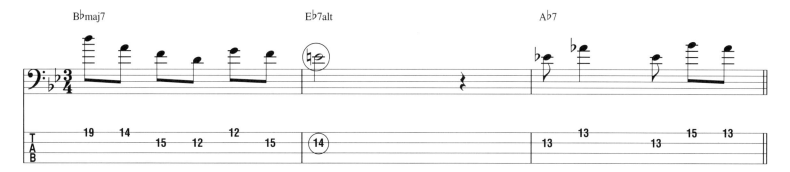

Here's another example of the same idea but this time using the ♭5th and ♯5th:

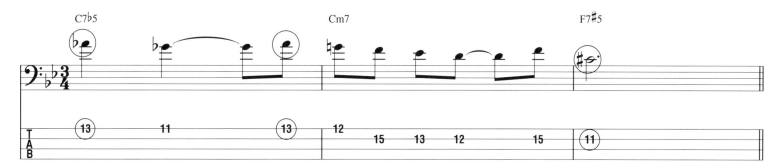

The next concept to consider is using scale fragments to travel from Point A to Point B. Rather than just randomly choosing from the altered scale, or playing it without a specific purpose, construct your melody with a destination note in mind.

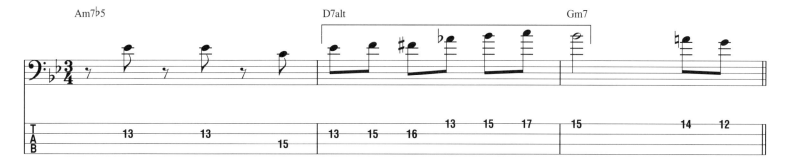

Scale fragments certainly aren't required to end or begin with altered tensions. Instead, the idea is to use the altered scale with a clear intention, as a way to move toward a melodic "goal."

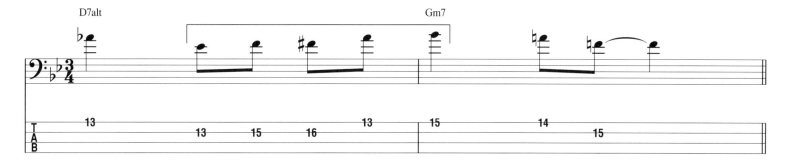

Finally, explore how you can use tension and release with alterations. There is a natural tension from the dissonance inherent in the altered dominant sound. Explore ways to play with that "friction" by incorporating both the altered sounds and the chord tones themselves.

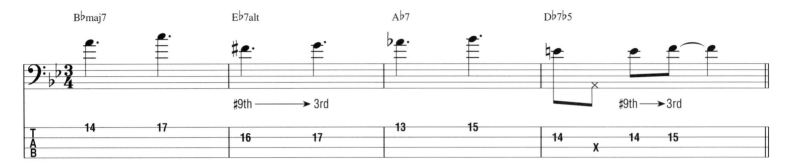

Now let's put all of this chapter's lessons (thumb-position technique, altered scales, cycle-of-4ths progressions, chords with altered 5ths, etc.) together in a solo example:

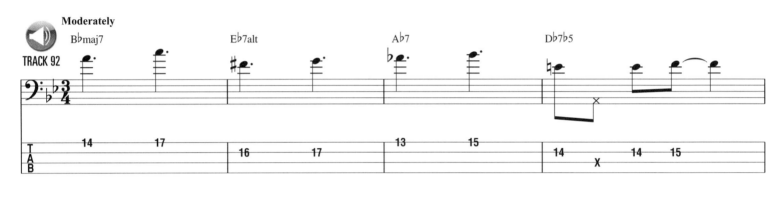

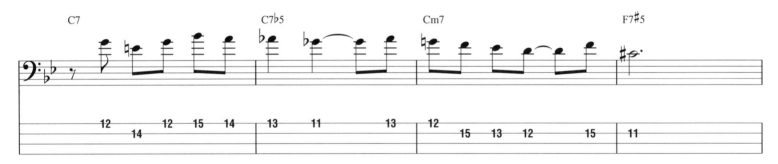

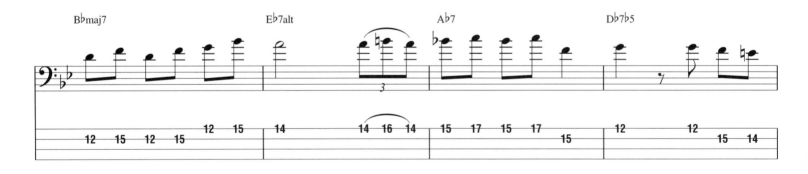

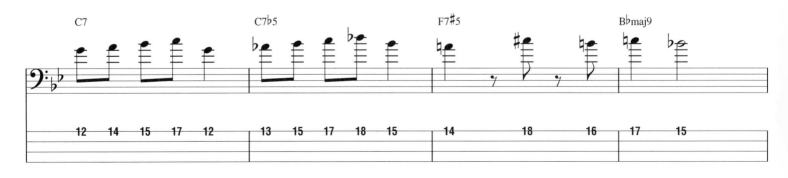

Keep these concepts and techniques in mind as we move into "bebop" in our next chapter.

CHAPTER 9

LIVING IN HARMONY: COMPOUND CHORDS

Compound chords, or "slash" chords, contain more than one element. Written as C/E ("C over E") or Cmaj7/B♭ ("C major seven over B♭"), for example, this spelling indicates the **voicing** of the chord ("voicing" refers to how the notes of a chord are distributed).

In our role as accompanists, bass players would focus first on the lower part of the slash chord (to the right of the slash), usually playing it on the downbeat if we're following the traditional walking bass line construction. Here's how the above examples look:

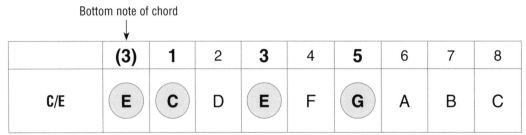

Our first example, C/E, would be considered an *inversion*, a chord voiced with a chord tone other than its root in the bass. Other examples of slash chords written as inversions are Cmaj7/E, C7/B♭, C7/G, etc.

The second example, Cmaj7/B♭, is a **hybrid slash chord**. This is a chord whose bass note is a non-chord tone. Other instances include C/F, Dm7/G, and G7/E.

The examples for this chapter's study will focus on the inversion type of slash chords, but we may see some hybrid chords in Chapter 10, so be on the lookout!

TECHNIQUE TUNE-UP: TWO-FINGER TECHNIQUE

While there's a lot of strength when correctly using one finger on our plucking hand, using two—either together or in alternation—greatly increases our ability to maneuver around the instrument and can even create a bigger sound. Here are some photos for reference:

Two Fingers Together

Alternating Two Fingers

Typical Position of Thumb

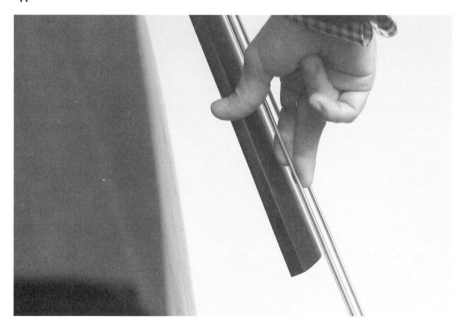

Standard Electric Position   **Typical Position of Thumb on Electric**

The following exercises use simple parameters to bring attention to this important rudimentary technique. Adding the second plucking finger greatly increases the variety of patterns to practice and enables us to perform a wider range of musical phrases.

The compound chords we just learned are great vehicles for two-finger practice, as they often contain different intervals than the ascending and descending major and minor 3rds that are in most chord spellings. But, first, let's begin with just open strings to get warmed up.

Slow

Plucking hand: 1   2   1   2   1   2   1   2   1 2 1 2 1 2 1 2   *sim.*

1 2 1 2 1 2 1 2 1 2 1 2 *sim.*   1 2 1 2 *sim.*

Next, incorporate alternate plucking fingerings:

Moderately

Plucking hand: 2   1   2   1   1   2   2   1   2   1   1   2   1   2   1   1

2   1   2   2   1   1   2   1   2   2   1   2   1   1   2   2

Now add string crossing to the mix by arpeggiating some compound chords:

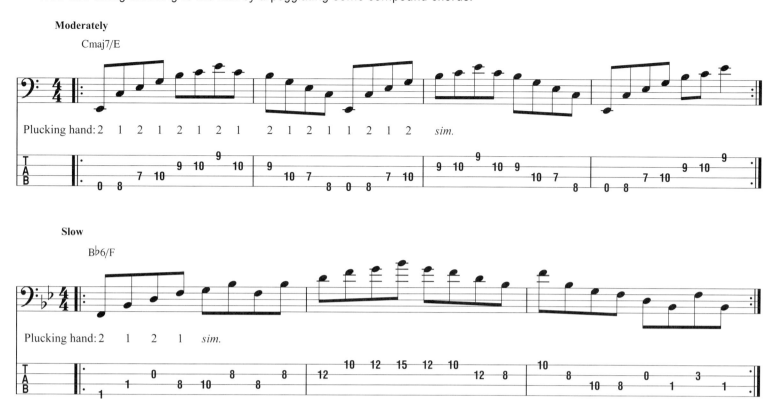

Lastly, add alternate fingering choices while crossing strings. Beginning some of these arpeggios with different plucking fingers might feel awkward, but this approach provides a good tool for refining our dexterity.

As always, incorporate these techniques into all of your other studies. For example, dedicate time to using two fingers as you learn a new song, melody, or solo.

We'll use this technique later on in this chapter, so keep it in mind as we now move on to studying another one of the most commonly used chord progressions, "rhythm changes."

CHANGES ARE INEVITABLE: RHYTHM CHANGES

The term **contrafact** refers to a musical composition with a new theme imposed on a familiar harmonic structure. For example, the melody to the classic cartoon "The Flintstones" is written over the same chord progression as the indelible song "I Got Rhythm," the focus of this section.

Written by George and Ira Gershwin, and published in 1930, the progression to "I Got Rhythm" has been the springboard for many jazz pieces that followed. Ironically, the original piece's final "A" section is ten bars long, as opposed to the ubiquitous eight-bar sections of nearly all the contrafacts. For our purpose, we'll use the common 32-bar AABA form that is played most often.

Containing I–vi–ii–V progressions, the cycle of 4ths, compound chords, passing diminished chords, and plenty of room for harmonic substitutions, **rhythm changes** are a fantastic vehicle for studying several aspects of jazz music.

Rhythm Changes in B♭

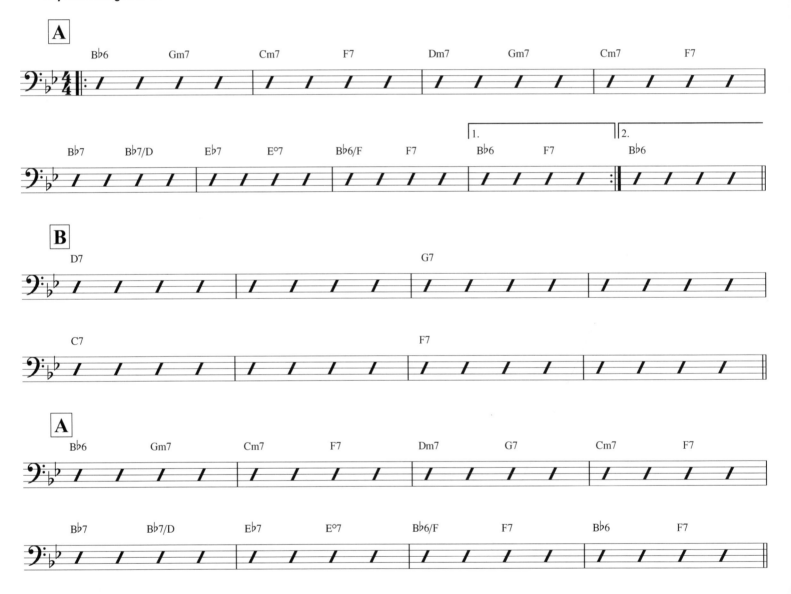

This 32-bar AABA form, in which each section is eight bars long, is exceedingly common in many jazz compositions.

In this specific chart, do you notice the I–vi–ii–V and iii–vi–ii–V progressions as the first four bars of the A sections? The bridge (B section) is a portion of the cycle of 4ths, and compound and passing diminished chords are present in the last four measures of each A section.

Let's do a basic arpeggiation of the progression slowly in time, using our two-finger technique. For demonstration purposes, let's observe just one A section.

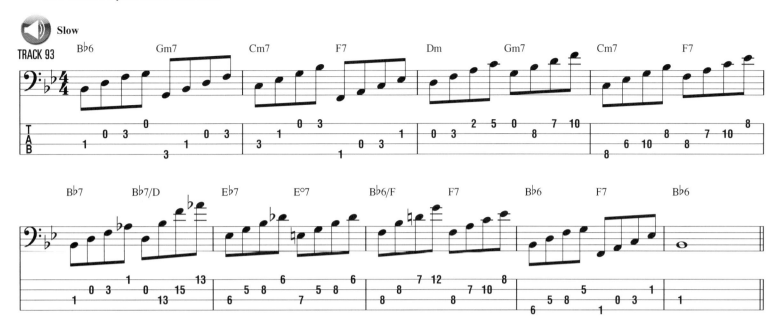

Now apply this exercise to the whole progression, using as many variations as you can come up with, like playing in different inversions, different arpeggio directions, and different rhythms.

Next, take a look at some very common ways that the basic chords are changed while maintaining the form and underlying harmonic structure. Pay attention to the chord qualities and strive to hear how they differ from our first example. Use the play-along track to practice creating your own walking bass lines.

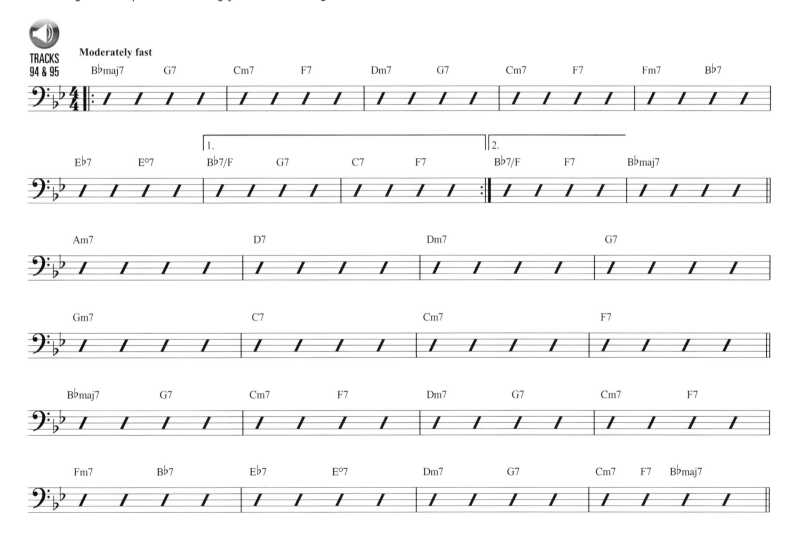

An extraordinarily powerful way of playing jazz developed in the late '30s and '40s and changed jazz forever. Come to be known as "bebop," Charlie Parker, Dizzy Gillespie, Thelonious Monk, and many other genius musicians manipulated existing concepts of rhythm, melody, and harmony to create something entirely new.

Bebop composers often used rhythm changes as the basis for their own contrafacts, and so bebop's melodic and rhythmic velocity and density, as well as its harmonic sophistication, became transferred onto the standard rhythm changes form. Check out some more ways to interpret rhythm changes below.

As mentioned, playing fast tempos is a common association with both rhythm changes and bebop. So, let's look at walking bass lines in this context in our next section.

BASS ACCOMPANIMENT: SPEED WALKING

Usually, the majority of your up-tempo playing will be accompanying others with walking bass lines. Although the rhythmic choices are primarily quarter notes, you need a tremendous amount of stamina and strength to withstand solo chorus after solo chorus. From my personal experience, the very best way to excel at walking fast tempos is to simply play them in a musical context as much as possible. Try them on gigs, in sessions with others, and with play-alongs.

One thing that I would suggest when practicing very fast walking is to really try to structure your perception of the time in bigger "chunks." So, rather than thinking 1–2–3–4 for every quarter note, think in whole measures: bar 1, bar 2, bar 3, etc.

Much of our struggle playing at high speeds is the ability to think quickly. Dedicated practice to expanding how fast we process and think ahead is invaluable. Additionally, it can extremely helpful to decide on good-sounding lines and prepare them ahead of time.

Another helpful tip to stay calm while playing "burning" tempos is to rely on some conventional devices to streamline your walking line. Repeated notes or patterns are very useful, as they can anchor the bass line for yourself and for others.

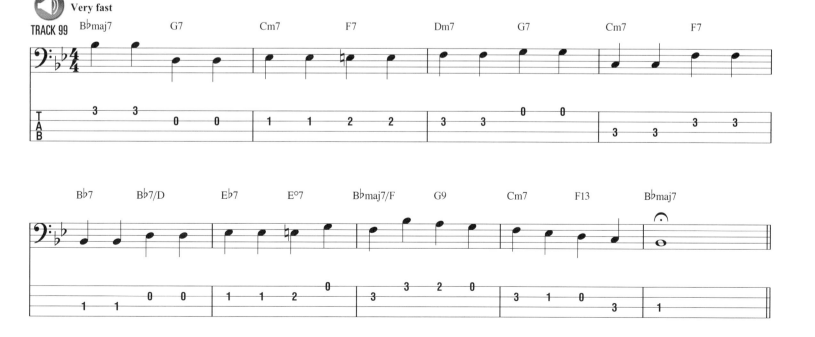

You can also practice a line or phrase faster than your intended speed. For example, after spending some time working hard to play a line at 300 BPM, suddenly playing it at 250 BPM becomes much more comfortable.

Below is a full chorus of rhythm changes recorded at 300 BPM. Use the play-along track to practice at a fast tempo and notice how your command of the time improves when you slow it down afterwards.

PREPARING TO SOLO: BEBOP SCALES

Over time, analysis of the music of bebop masters lead to a codification of a new series of scales—**bebop scales**. Incorporating set passing tones between specific scale degrees, the bebop scales tend to be played in such a way that the passing notes connect strong beats in a bar. However, careful listening and studying on your own will teach you more than any book ever will.

The first scale, usually called the bebop scale, is bebop dominant. The **bebop dominant scale** is the Mixolydian mode with a passing tone between the ♭7th and the root.

C Bebop Dominant Scale

There is also a **bebop minor scale**, or "bebop Dorian," with a passing tone between the minor 3rd and 4th of the scale.

C Bebop Minor Scale

Not to be outdone, major scales also have their own bebop variation, the **bebop major scale**, with an extra passing tone between the 5th and 6th of the major scale. Major sixth and major seventh chords are usually the place where this is used.

C Bebop Major Scale

The **bebop harmonic minor scale** has an additional ♭7th between the ♭6th and ♮7th of the regular harmonic minor scale. This can be used over all three chords of a minor ii–V–i progression.

C Bebop Harmonic Minor Scale

Lastly, the melodic minor scale has a corresponding bebop arrangement, the **bebop melodic minor scale**, with a chromatic passing tone between the 5th and 6th. It's usually used over minor sixth chords.

C Bebop Melodic Minor Scale

ALL EARS ON YOU: HEIGHTEN YOUR MOBILITY

When we improvise, thinking and hearing both clearly and quickly is a valuable asset. Just as we practice available note choices for our walking bass lines in such a way that we're able to perceive many note options within one bar, we should also strive to become very "mobile" in our improvised melodies. This general concept is not new, but I must give credit for this exercise to pianist David Berkman and his great book *The Jazz Musician's Guide to Creative Practicing*.

Our goal in this section's "workout" is to train ourselves to quickly adjust our available note choices as chord changes pass in time. In other words, we want to have quick access to many options as we improvise. This ability comes from slow practice outside of the performance moment, but the crux of the exercise is to both open up and strengthen our command of possibilities.

We'll use the bebop scales we just learned in the context of rhythm changes. Understand that this is intended as a learning tool, and not as a direct way to build good melodies. In other words, these aren't licks, but rather a way of practicing.

We'll play through the chord changes with steady rhythms. We'll start from a particular note, usually high or low on the instrument, and continue up and down, reversing direction when notes get too high or too low. We'll gradually increase the rhythmic density and speed and change starting notes as we progress.

The first step in this process is to choose the scales that we'll use over all of the chords. We want to set parameters for ourselves so that we can focus on the idea, rather than spending time in the moment searching for choices.

You can make the scale-to-chord choices anything you want, but in this exercise, we'll use the following:

- **For dominant chords:** bebop dominant
- **For major chords:** bebop major
- **For minor chords:** bebop minor
- **For diminished chords:** half-whole diminished

Next, play through the form of the song out of time, following the chord progression. Each time you encounter a new chord, play the appropriate scale up and down, thinking about the scale you're currently playing and the scale you'll play next. (For the sake of space, we'll just use the first two measures of rhythm changes to demonstrate.)

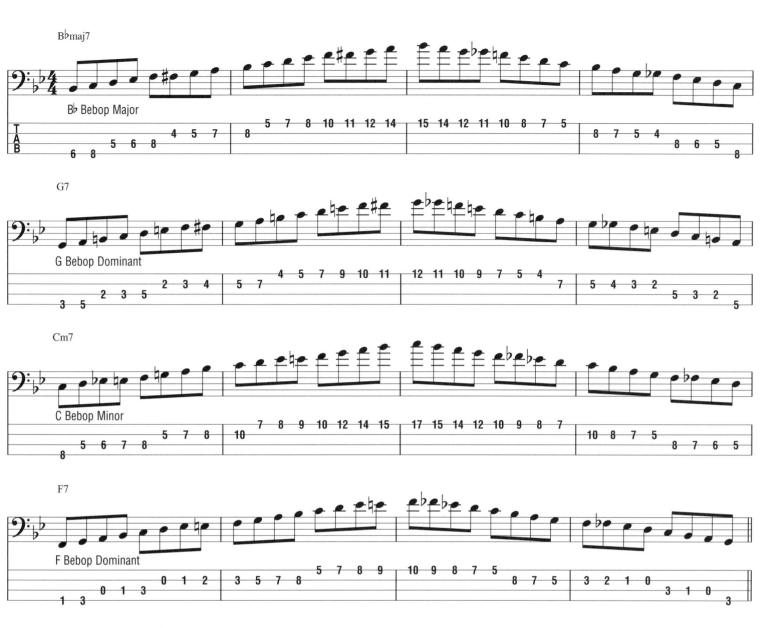

Now set your first rhythmic parameters by using continuous quarter notes, like a walking bass line. However, instead of playing the root when the chord changes, *play the closest note from the corresponding scale that continues in the direction of the line.* When we start from a Bb on the Bbmaj7 chord, the closest note of the G bebop dominant scale that maintains the ascending line is E♮ (the harmonic rhythm is still stretched here).

Apply the same principle moving forward, but begin the pattern on a *different starting note*. It can be any note in the appropriate chord scale, but for this part, I like to play the lowest note on the instrument that's in the scale.

Next, let's play the correct harmonic rhythm.

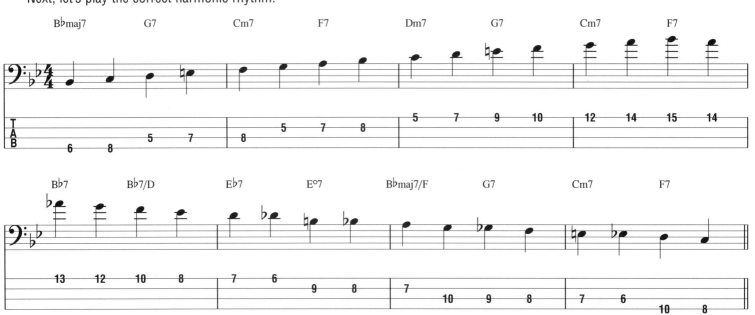

Now let's move to an eighth-note rhythm and play at a specific tempo.

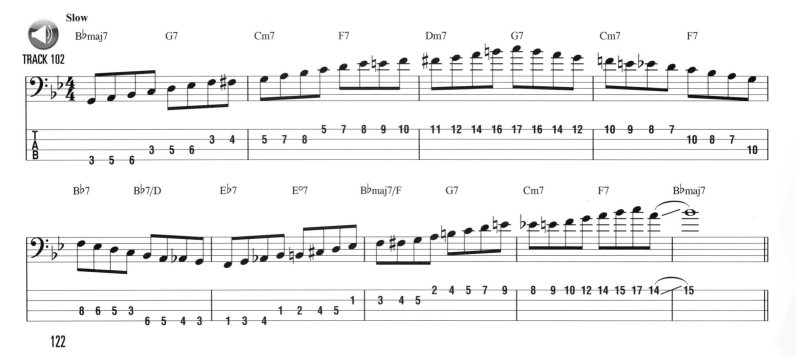

Finally, increase the tempo and rhythmic value. For example, here is the same section of rhythm changes but with a faster tempo and 16th-note rhythm:

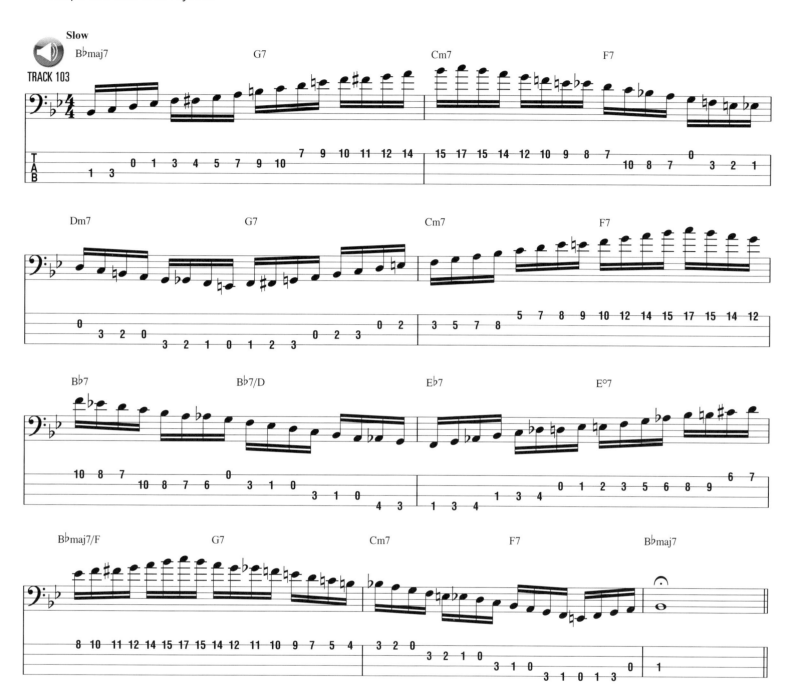

Be sure to spend time fleshing out this whole idea with the full form of rhythm changes, and then apply it to other songs that you know or are learning. I've found this incredibly rewarding in my own practice!

CHAPTER 10

LIVING IN HARMONY: HYBRID CHORDS

The last three types of chords that we'll examine in this book are hybrid chords, minor-major seventh chords, and "add" chords. Moving forward, every chord that you encounter in your musical life will be some derivation of the types of chords that we've encountered in this book. For example, a C6/9 chord is a C6 chord with an added 9th. You can apply all of the concepts that we've learned to any chord that you see or hear.

Hybrid chords, sometimes called "polychords," are a type of compound chord. They are constructed by stacking one complete chord (triad, seventh, etc.) on top of another. One way to differentiate them from other compound chords is that you'll notice a straight, horizontal line between the chords, rather than an angled slash.

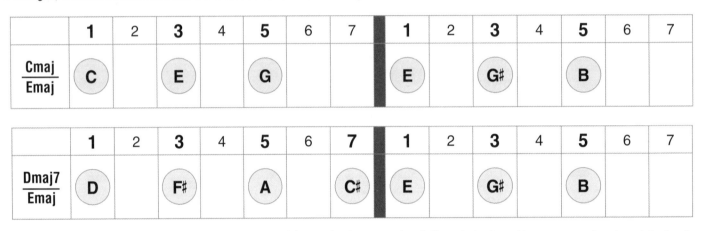

Generally speaking, we, as bass players, would address the bottom chord first, but since there are no hard-and-fast rules about how to approach these chords, this can be flexible. You'll also notice that the other notes of the corresponding scales are absent in the graphics above since they are dependent on the particular composer's or improviser's intent. Your default choices can still be the standard chord scales, should you be unclear as to what that intent is.

Minor-major seventh chords are exactly what they sound like—a four-part chord with a minor triad and a major 7th. Derived from either the harmonic minor or melodic minor scale, you can use either scale for improvising.

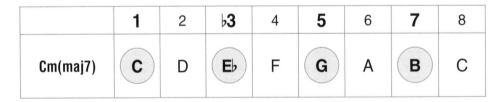

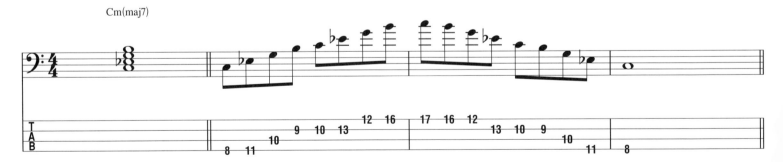

Add chords are basic triads with one additional note. A Cadd2 chord, for example, is a basic C triad with an added D—the 2nd of the scale. Because these added notes are non-chord tones, the other options you'll see are "add4" and "add6." Sometimes, you may see the added note as a tension (add9, add11, or add13), meaning it's above the octave of the root.

	1	2	3	4	5	6	7	8
Cadd2	C	D	E	F	G	A	B	C

TECHNIQUE TUNE-UP: BEAT MANIPULATION

In your listening, you've probably heard many examples of beat manipulation. Some players tend to play "on top" of the beat, while others play behind or right on the beat. As bassists, because we are constantly playing throughout a performance, we are also constantly negotiating the time feel between ourselves and the other musicians. Therefore, it's important to have an awareness of the different ways of playing the time, and having control of our own placement of rhythm is fundamental to our job.

To review, take a look at the graphic below, which helps to visualize the different ways of playing. Each circle represents a unit of rhythm, like a quarter note, where we can identify three sections of each beat.

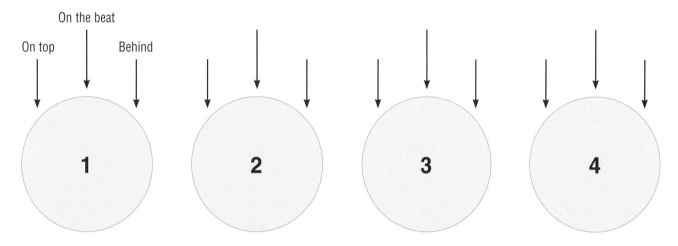

Each arrow represents the location where we would consistently place our attack in the context of an objective, metronomic beat. So, to play *on the beat* would be to play precisely in time with the metronome. Playing *on top* of the beat means playing on the front part of that objective beat and gives the music a sense of urgency or intensity. "Laying back," or playing *behind* the beat, evokes a more relaxed feeling.

Listen to and play along with the examples below, where my fantastic colleagues, Oscar Perez (piano) and Ulysses Owens, Jr. (drums), and I demonstrate the three types of beat management. The first example is played behind the beat, the second example is played on the beat, and the third example is played on top of the beat.

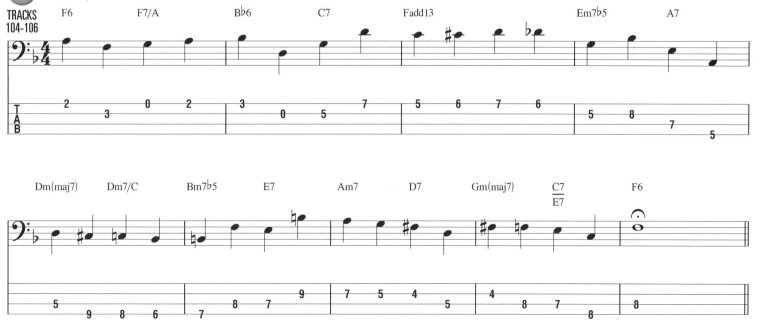

A compelling way to use this rhythmic control is to place phrases or overall time feels against a contrasting feeling. In the examples below, you'll see "lay back" directives, where the phrases pull against the time feel that is currently defining the excerpt.

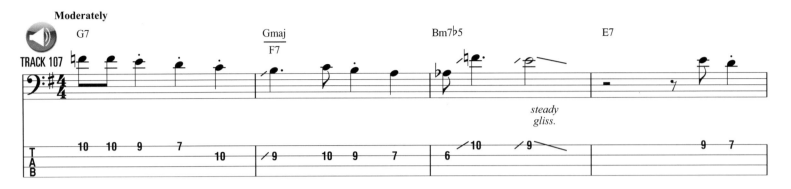

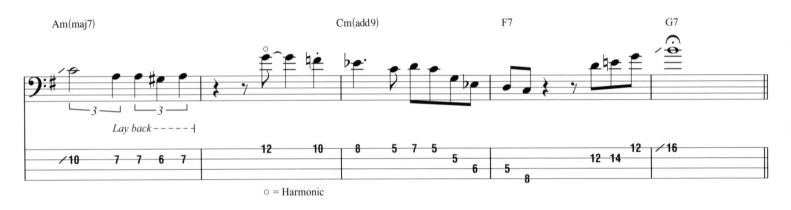

○ = Harmonic

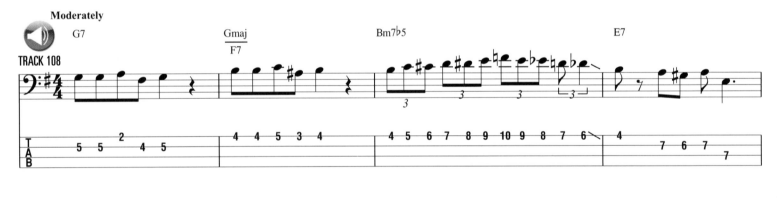

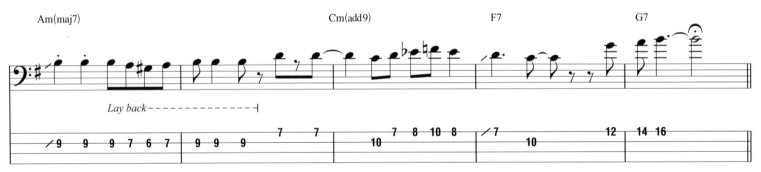

This is just a small sample of the ways in which we can use beat manipulation. Listen to the great musicians of yesterday and today and take special notice of where and how they control the beat. Mastering this skill takes time, but the effort is well worth it. Good luck!

CHANGES ARE INEVITABLE: MODAL PROGRESSIONS

Modal jazz is music whose harmonic framework is based on modes rather than traditional chord progressions. While the chords we've learned are used in these kinds of compositions, there are some general characteristics that tend to be indicative of modal tunes.

Often, the harmonic rhythm is quite long and chords go unchanged for many measures. The harmonic function typically found in other compositions can be "suppressed" or hidden, and there is often more use of polytonality in modal tunes. Pedal points, which we'll explore later in this chapter, are also more common in modal music, as are ostinatos.

The most recognizable examples of modal jazz are found in works by Miles Davis, John Coltrane, Woody Shaw, and Herbie Hancock, among others. Songs like Davis' "So What" (from *Kind of Blue*) and Hancock's "Maiden Voyage" are quintessential modal compositions.

In fact, the chord progression to "So What" is used in a variety of well-known songs, including Coltrane's "Impressions" and Freddie Hubbard's "Little Sunflower." Miles' intention with *Kind of Blue* was to allow his group to superimpose their own improvisational conceptions in music with a less "constraining" harmonic progression. Here's an example:

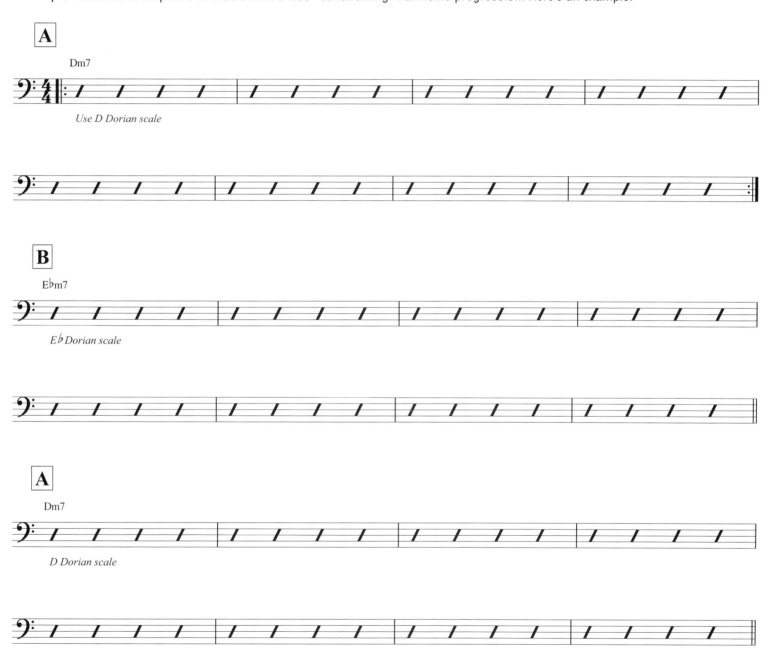

As bassists, we also have some freedom to impose some harmony on this relatively static progression. We'll explore this later, but suffice it to say, modal tunes are great ways to experiment with walking bass line chord substitutions.

While the progression shown on the previous page is a clear example of a modal tune, there are innumerable variations that still fit the overall concept. Below is another example, which we'll continue to work with later in this chapter.

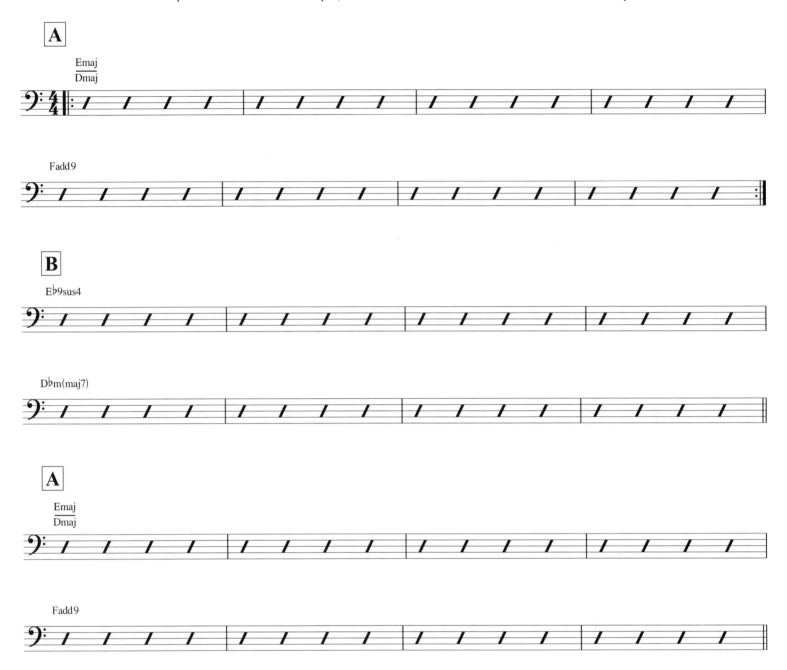

The modal concept encourages musicians to have freedom, but within a certain structure. Our next section touches on this idea, as well.

BASS ACCOMPANIMENT: PEDAL POINT

The kinds of bass lines that we've looked at so far tend to have a lot of forward movement. Conversely, ostinatos and pedal points are two techniques that have more of a fixed, or static, feeling. Ironically, this can lead to a *less* stable harmonic sense, since there is often movement in the harmony while the bass stays in one place.

An ostinato, as you may recall from Chapter 5, both "grounds" the rhythm and pulls against moving harmony. Taking a one- or two-bar bass line and repeating it over and over will provide a natural sense of stability against consonant harmony, and tension and release against dissonant sounds.

Let's play an ostinato figure, using the modal changes from the previous section. Listen to the effect on the music.

TRACK 109

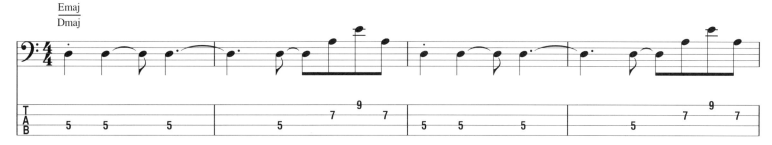

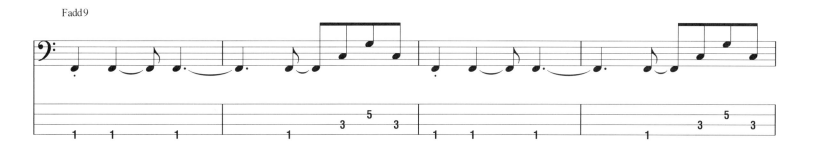

Conversely, playing a **pedal point** isn't about repeating a pattern of notes, but rather focusing on using one note as an underlying "drone" of sorts. "Pedaling" means that, whether by our own intention or that of the composer, we play a single pitch against all of the other harmony. To demonstrate this, let's use the rhythm from the previous example, but choose a single note for the whole exercise. In this case our pedal point is E:

TRACK 110

Do you notice how the sound of the repetitive E note against the different harmonies creates varying amounts of tension and release? This is the purpose of pedal point, though it doesn't mean it has to occur throughout a whole song. On the contrary, it usually occurs in one or more smaller portions of the overall form.

These basic principles are rarely more complicated than our examples above, though the variety of rhythms and note choices can cover a lot of sonic ground. However, it's not an inherently complex idea, and you should feel free to experiment with these ideas as much as you can.

In our next section, we'll investigate how we might choose melody notes for hybrid, minor-major seventh, and add chords.

PREPARING TO SOLO:
CONVENTIONAL CHORD SCALES FOR UNCONVENTIONAL CHORDS

Thankfully, we've already learned what we need to know to play over the add chords, polychords, and minor-major seventh chords that are the focus of this chapter. However, there are a couple ways to use this knowledge in our approach to improvising over them.

Polychords are the hardest to pin down, as the options for melodies vary according to the context, chord spelling, and possible harmonic function.

The first option we can use is to choose the specific notes that are indicated by the two chords and think of those as a "scale" of sorts. We're essentially just arpeggiating the triads.

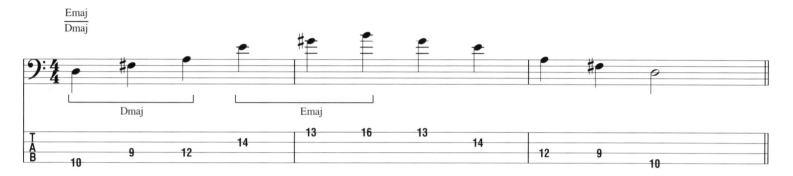

Expanding on this idea, we can experiment with extending the implied chord quality of the triads. For the example above, let's superimpose the major 7ths onto the two parts of the polychord:

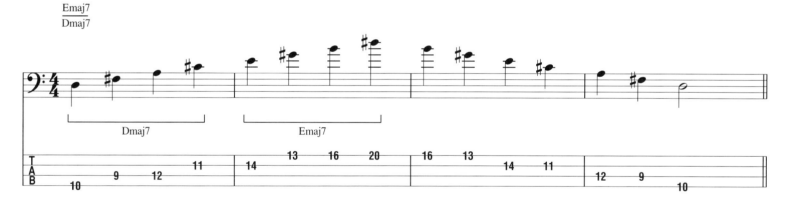

We can also analyze the progression and see if the polychord acts directly as a chord with a harmonic function (like a resolving dominant seventh chord) or can be "replaced" by a similar chord that does have a harmonic function. In our example below, the chord might be thought of as a tonic—perhaps a Dmaj7#11—over which we can play the Lydian mode.

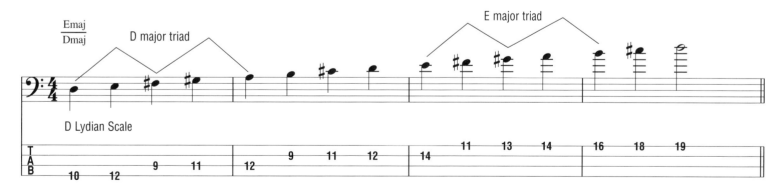

For add chords, as with any other harmony, our first option for improvisation is to utilize the notes in the chord spelling itself. Besides these, we can apply others in the scale from which the chord is derived. For instance, for an add chord based off a major triad (Cadd2, Cadd13), an option would be to employ the major scale.

Likewise, for minor add chords, we could employ the notes of any minor scale that fits with both the indicated harmonic structure and our musical intent.

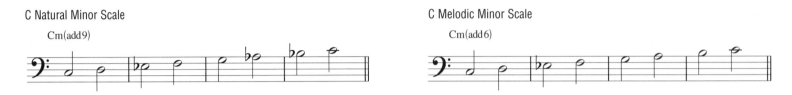

Lastly, minor-major seventh chords have a variety of options, but our first choices should be the fundamental harmonic minor or melodic minor scale. The scales naturally contain the ♭3rd and ♮7th, and so are a great place to start.

As with all improvising, be sure to take ample time to understand and experiment with all of these concepts.

For our very last section of the book, let's use the ideas above as we discuss soloing one more time.

ALL EARS ON YOU: UPPER-STRUCTURE TRIADS

Upper-structure triads are created by building chords on the notes of the chord scale above the root. Essentially, you are building triads from within the chord scale.

For a Cmaj7 chord, for example, where we are using the Ionian mode as the chord scale, a G major triad can be created from the 5th of C (G), the major 7th of C (B), and the tension 9th of C (D). Perhaps it may help to see it visually:

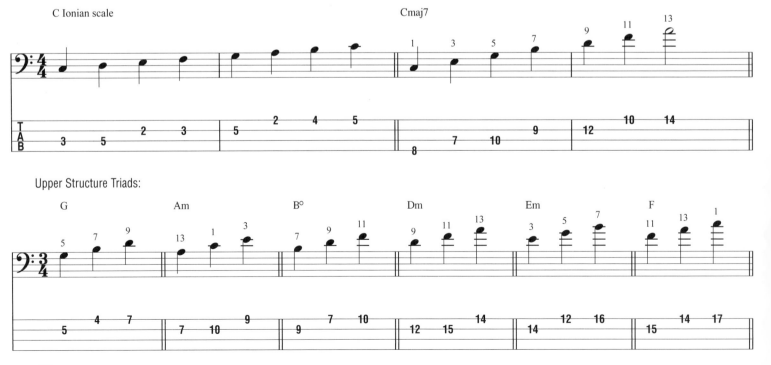

So, let's begin to think about applying this to improvisation. First off, we'll need to choose the chord scales for each chord in the progression that we are working on. Here are some options:

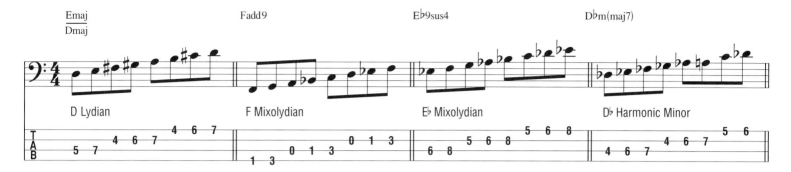

Now that we have chosen our chord scales, let's decide which upper-structure triads we will use. Write these triads above the original chord. Often, the major triad options will sound good because they have a clarity that sticks out, but other options are equally valid. Experiment with different options and find a sound that you like.

Take a small rhythmic motif and repeat it for each bar, changing triads as the harmony changes:

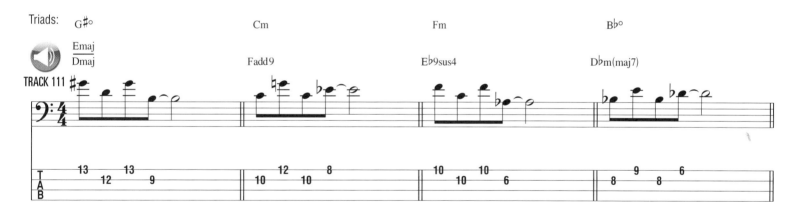

Now create a more organic solo, but still restrict your note choices to only the predetermined upper-structure triads. Work on making smooth connections between the changes, even within the limits of these triads.

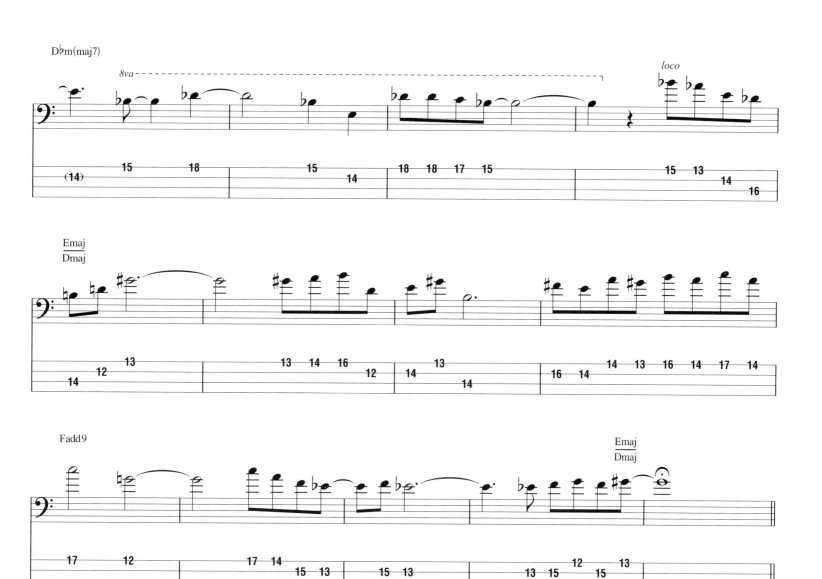

Once you have become comfortable limiting yourself to the upper structures, apply the idea to your normal soloing. You'll find interesting ideas for melodies with this technique. There are many options to delve into and I hope that you enjoy your journey as you find new sounds to make your own.

EPILOGUE

Congratulations! You're now well on your way to jazz mastery, should you choose to take that path. I sincerely hope that you've gotten a wealth of information from this method book, and that you will continue to explore the many aspects of jazz and music that we didn't have the opportunity to cover here.

There's a lifetime of learning in this music, so be patient and kind to yourself along the way. If I can be of personal assistance to you in some way, feel free to reach out to me via my website (matthewrybickimusic.com) or social media.

Thank you, once again, and as the jazz masters used to say, "Straight ahead and strive for tone!"

Warm wishes,
Matthew Rybicki

ABOUT THE AUTHOR

Raised in Cleveland, Ohio, Matthew Rybicki has performed with Wynton Marsalis and the Jazz at Lincoln Center Orchestra, Ernie Watts, Laurence Hobgood, Hilary Kole, Wycliffe Gordon, Ted Rosenthal, Mark Gould, Nnenna Freelon, Renee Fleming, Terell Stafford, Winard Harper, Mark Whitfield, Victor Goines, and Marcus Printup. He has also had the great fortune of performing at many well-respected venues in New York, including the Village Vanguard and the Blue Note, as well as concert halls and festivals in locations ranging from Italy to Qatar to Taiwan. Rybicki maintains an active performing schedule, working with his own ensembles and with many accomplished colleagues and mentors, including Lew Tabackin, Lewis Nash, Dan Nimmer, Oscar Perez, Christian Sands, Gerald Clayton, David Berger, and Charenee Wade.

An adept educator, Matthew holds a faculty position at the Juilliard School and is an artist/instructor for Jazz at Lincoln Center where he developed and taught the inaugural bass course in the Essentially Ellington Band Director Academy. He has also been the music director for several educational performance initiatives, including Jazz in the Schools and hospital tours in conjunction with Lincoln Center for the Performing Arts' Department of Services for People with Disabilities. In addition, Rybicki was a program coordinator for Midori and Friends and has led musical workshops at both the Whitney Museum of American Art and the Guggenheim, where he designed and presented educational performances that incorporate jazz with fine art.

Matthew has presented educational clinics in a wide variety of settings worldwide. Highlights include master-classes and clinics at the International Society of Bassists Annual Convention (Rochester, NY), Qatar Music Academy (Doha, Qatar), The Vitoria Jazz Festival (Vitoria, Spain), Georgia State University (Atlanta, GA), Snow College (Ephraim, UT), Centro Nacional de las Artes (Mexico City, Mexico), Spoleto Music Festival (Spoleto, Italy), and The National Jazz Museum in Harlem (New York, NY).

He has also authored books for Hal Leonard, including *Ray Brown: Legendary Jazz Bassist*, and co-authored *Bass Lesson Goldmine: 100 Jazz Lessons*, both of which were released in 2015.

Driven, Rybicki's debut recording released in 2009, allowed him to be formally acknowledged on the jazz scene as a performer and composer of note. Recording with jazz greats Ron Blake, Freddie Hendrix, Gerald Clayton, and Ulysses Owens, he was able to capture innovative and sophisticated performances of newly created original works that maintain close ties to the history of jazz.

Matthew received his Artist Diploma graduate degree from the Juilliard School in 2004 and his Bachelor of Music from Berklee College of Music in 1995.